Bewilderment

Bewilderment
A spiritual companion

Robert Atwell

CANTERBURY
PRESS

© Robert Atwell 2025

Published in 2025 by Canterbury Press
Editorial office
3rd Floor, Invicta House,
110 Golden Lane,
London EC1Y 0TG, UK
www.canterburypress.co.uk

Canterbury Press is an imprint of Hymns Ancient & Modern Ltd
(a registered charity)

Hymns Ancient & Modern® is a registered trademark of
Hymns Ancient & Modern Ltd
13A Hellesdon Park Road, Norwich,
Norfolk NR6 5DR, UK

All rights reserved. No part of this publication may be reproduced,
stored in a retrieval system, or transmitted,
in any form or by any means, electronic, mechanical,
photocopying or otherwise, without the prior permission of
the publisher, Canterbury Press.

Robert Atwell has asserted his right under the Copyright, Designs and
Patents Act 1988 to be identified as the Author of this Work

Apart from the Psalms, Scripture quotations are from the New Revised
Standard Version Bible: Anglicized Edition, copyright © 1989, 1995 National
Council of the Churches of Christ in the United States of America. Used by
permission. All rights reserved worldwide.

Quotations of the Psalms are taken from the Psalter in *Common Worship: Services
and Prayers for the Church of England*, copyright © 2000 The Archbishops' Council
of the Church of England. Used by permission. All rights reserved worldwide.

978 1-78622-647-1

British Library Cataloguing in Publication data
A catalogue record for this book is available
from the British Library

EU GPSR Authorised Representative
LOGOS EUROPE, 9 rue Nicolas Poussin, 17000, LA ROCHELLE, France
E-mail: Contact@logoseurope.eu

Typeset by Regent Typesetting
Based on the design of the author's earlier book *The Contented Life*
(Canterbury Press, 2011), by Christina Forde.

Contents

Acknowledgements	ix
Introduction	xi
1 Signs of the times	1
2 The reluctant prophet	21
3 The right road lost	41
4 Out of the depths	57
5 Not waving but drowning	71
6 Down and out in Nineveh	83
7 The God who provides	95
8 The God of compassion and love	105
Epilogue	119
Acknowledgements of Copyright Sources	121
List of Illustrations	122
Notes	123

To the clergy and people of the Diocese of Exeter
in thanksgiving for our partnership in the gospel

Acknowledgements

I am indebted to Canon Vincent Strudwick, who read and commented on the script during the writing, and to the Reverend Canon Professor Sue Gillingham, Emeritus Professor of the Hebrew Bible, Emeritus Fellow of Worcester College, Oxford and Canon Theologian of Exeter Cathedral, for her perceptive observations on the Hebrew text.

Some of the scribes and Pharisees said to Jesus, 'Teacher, we wish to see a sign from you.' But he answered them, 'An evil and adulterous generation asks for a sign, but no sign will be given to it except the sign of the prophet Jonah. For just as Jonah was for three days and three nights in the belly of the sea monster, so for three days and three nights the Son of Man will be in the heart of the earth. The people of Nineveh will rise up at the judgement with this generation and condemn it, because they repented at the proclamation of Jonah, and see, something greater than Jonah is here! The queen of the South will rise up at the judgement with this generation and condemn it, because she came from the ends of the earth to listen to the wisdom of Solomon, and see, something greater than Solomon is here!'

Matthew 12.38–42 (Luke 11.29–32)

Introduction

This book grew out of a series of Quiet Days I led for the clergy of the Diocese of Exeter during my time as Bishop of Exeter. It is written in counterpoint. Chapters alternate between observations on the challenges facing Christian discipleship in an era of unprecedented change, and reflections on an undervalued book of the Bible, that of the prophet Jonah.

Jonah occupies a unique place in the Hebrew canon of Scripture. It is listed among the so-called Twelve Minor (shorter) Prophets, but some commentators wonder what on earth it is doing in the Bible. It is unusual because it is not a collection of prophecies or oracles, but a colourful story about a reluctant prophet who initially rejects the call of God and runs away. In the end he grits his teeth and successfully summons an entire city of foreigners to repentance but promptly goes into a sulk – not because his preaching was a disaster but because it was a success, and God does not destroy the city of Nineveh as he had secretly hoped.

Jonah is the only Jew in the story, but through him Gentiles are saved: first the crew of a ship bound for the port of Tarshish and then the people of Nineveh, the capital of the Assyrian Empire. The city was hated and feared in equal measure in the ancient world because of the cruelty the Ninevites habitually inflicted on those they conquered. The tensions and hatreds across today's Middle East have a long and disturbing history. Set against a dark backcloth of conquest and violence, Jonah is a story about forgiveness and repentance. It is a story about God's boundless love, mercy and compassion, which we learn embraces not just human beings but the entire created order.

Mention the name of Jonah and most people (at least those with a rudimentary knowledge of the Bible) immediately think of whales and sea monsters. They either dismiss it as a fairy tale or view it through spectacles coloured by the film *Jaws*. They latch on to the bizarre elements of the story and neglect what is in fact a profound piece of writing. Jonah is a radical protest book, taking an apparently pious individual and turning everything upside down. There are undoubtedly elements of Hebrew folklore in the story, but this does not mean that we should regard it with suspicion. Anthropologists of religion have shown that folklore is a powerful way of communicating beliefs about God and the nature of the world we inhabit. Jesus certainly had no hesitation in referring to Jonah, and toyed with various aspects of the story, using Jonah's time in the belly of the whale as an image of his own imminent death and burial. He applauds Jonah's preaching to the people of Nineveh, but says intriguingly: 'And I tell you, something greater than Jonah is here.'

I have always been fascinated by the story of Jonah. It caught my imagination as a child, as evidently it also did the first Christians. When I was a student, I was amazed to discover frescoes of Jonah dating from the fourth century painted on the walls and ceilings of the catacombs in Rome, such as those in the catacomb of Marcellinus and Peter on the ancient Via Labricana. Jonah is depicted boarding a ship, being thrown into a raging sea by terrified sailors, and being swallowed by a large fish. Another fresco shows him being spewed out of the mouth of the whale and preaching to the Ninevites. Yet another has him sitting under a makeshift shelter of branches as he awaits the destruction of their city. Because Jonah was in the belly of the fish 'three days and three nights' and because Jesus links this with his own

Catacomb of Marcellinus and Peter: Jonah thrown into the sea to be swallowed by a large fish, and spewed out near the city of Nineveh.

death, the early Christians saw in Jonah's story a foretelling of Christ's resurrection. Jonah was seen as heralding the salvation brought by Christ and his descent into the water as an image of baptism. Jonah became a figure of hope in the face of death and destruction.

As someone who cannot swim a stroke and who enjoys looking at the sea but not being in it, I have always been in awe of Jonah. He is admittedly an unlikely hero, and my admiration is eccentric. After all, we like to picture the prophets as strong, confident figures and Jonah is neither of these. He is a flawed individual, at times almost comic. He certainly stands apart from the other Hebrew prophets, particularly Obadiah and Nahum, who loathed everything Nineveh stood for and were uncompromising in their condemnation of its tyranny. After their violent denunciations, Jonah's story comes as a welcome relief and, as we shall see, a bit of a surprise. It is why I find Jonah such an attractive character. He is irascible, vulnerable, moody and disobedient, but he is also honest and courageous, qualities that are often overlooked.

I am not a biblical scholar, and I write as a Christian reader of a Jewish book. But I hope my observations about both Jonah and the challenges facing us today will enable a new generation to reconnect with this ancient text and discover wisdom. Each chapter concludes with a series of questions or suggestions for prayer to stimulate personal reflection. If this book is being used in a study or Lent group, the questions could be used or adapted to prompt discussion.

We live in turbulent times. Our era is marked by confusion, fear and anxiety. One of the things that has led me to revisit this extraordinary story is Jonah's evident fear and bewilderment in the face of the events that confronted his generation. One biblical commentator, the Dominican Paul Murray, goes so far as to describe the book as a theological exploration of bewilderment.[1] I have never had a great conversion moment or enjoyed the intense spiritual experiences that some of my friends describe, so I warm to Paul Murray's description. In my spiritual life I have just bumbled along, often stumbling in the process. As I grapple with the call of Jesus Christ to follow him, I continue to take comfort in a verse in the psalms: 'Though you stumble, you shall not fall headlong, for the Lord holds you fast by the hand' (Psalm 37.24). This book is written for my fellow bumblers and stumblers.

In his play *A Man for All Seasons*, Robert Bolt puts into the mouth of the play's hero, Sir Thomas More, these words: 'God made the angels to show him splendour, as he made animals for innocence and plants for their simplicity. But man he made to serve him wittily, in the tangle of his mind.'[2] Who knows? Perhaps in our current bewilderment, in the tangle of our mind, Jonah may have unexpected things to say to our generation.

Ours is a time of anxiety because we have willed it to be so. Our anxiety is not imposed on us by force from outside. We impose it on our world and upon one another from within ourselves.

Thomas Merton (1915–68)
Thoughts in Solitude

1
Signs of the times

'Sign' is an important word in the New Testament. St Paul points to 'signs' that he performed and argues that they support his claim to be a 'true apostle'.[3] The fourth Evangelist uses the word to denote key events in the life of Jesus that 'revealed his glory', and in the Synoptic Gospels we encounter the Pharisees and Sadducees badgering Jesus for 'a sign'. They seek demonstrable evidence that would authenticate his alleged divine authority.[4] Jesus refuses to kowtow to their demand and mysteriously refers to 'the sign of Jonah', linking Jonah's time in the belly of the whale with his own imminent death and burial. On another occasion he ridicules his critics for their ability to spot changes in the clouds that signal a change in the weather, but their inability to interpret the movements and events in the world around them: 'You know how to interpret the appearance of the sky, but you cannot interpret the signs of the times.'[5]

What in our generation are the 'signs of the times' and how do we understand them? What is the 'sign of Jonah' and how might it shape our discipleship? These are questions I want to explore.

A new 'Age of Anxiety'

Historians of Late Antiquity, the period from the end of the third century to the seventh century, call it the 'Age of Anxiety'.[6] The western Roman Empire fell apart. The road system, which had guaranteed the swift and safe movement of food, troops and commerce throughout the empire, was no longer being properly maintained. People became reluctant to travel because they no longer felt safe. There was a loss of confidence in civic life. Cities were becoming lawless. Families began to move out of the towns and seek refuge on country estates, many of which became fortified enclosures. Rumours of barbarian incursions caused widescale panic. With the forces of chaos at the gates of Rome, civilization was under threat.

Parallels with our own age are not hard to draw. There is increasing lawlessness on our streets. Anxious middle-class citizens live in electronically gated enclaves, miniature stockades to keep 'undesirables' at bay. In many countries, including our own, there has been a collapse of trust in government and politicians, and a shift of attitudes towards previously trusted institutions such as the police and media. Fewer people bother to vote in general and local elections, and the government is worried about the decline of social capital, the glue that holds society together.[7] The smell of social and institutional decay is in the air. Although we are more protected and secure than earlier generations – and enjoy a higher standard of living than our grandparents, with better medicine, safer transport and social security – public confidence remains fragile. Many have yet to recover from the trauma of the Covid pandemic. There is unease about immigration in general and asylum seekers in particular, who are seen as threatening community cohesion. Meanwhile, climate change, the territorial and economic ambitions of the superpowers, the intractable and incendiary conflicts of the Middle East, and the manipulation of trust on social media combine to generate a heady mix of uncertainty and fear. Cyber-attacks and international terrorism, dark forces intent on causing havoc, threaten our way of life. We find ourselves living in a second 'Age of Anxiety'.

Commenting on the post-Cold War situation in 1993, Samuel P. Huntington, the American political theorist, predicted a 'clash of civilizations'.[8] He argued that future wars would be fought not between nation states but between cultures – except nation states continue to lock horns. There has been a resurgence of nationalism, and power-hungry autocrats are not in short supply. That said, the cultural tectonic plates are undoubtedly shifting. We are witnessing the end of the post-colonial era and the end of a dominant North American/European way of understanding and ordering the world, and it is producing waves of anxiety. For many people and for a variety of reasons, the future isn't what it used to be. Populism is on the rise. People feel bewildered and frightened, if not for themselves then for their children.

Living with change

Living with flux and uncertainty are facts of life in the twenty-first century, exacerbated by the speed of technological change. Artificial Intelligence (AI) is generating a raft of exciting possibilities that in time could improve efficiency and solve many of our problems. But no new technology is without its shadow side, and the problems it creates as well as the ones it solves need to be addressed. In the experience of some, the relentless promotion of AI is accompanied by the presumption that what is new or what is next must be better, and it ratchets up the pressure. Companies go out of business if they fail to keep up, nations are left behind, individuals become exhausted.

If you need just one example of the extraordinary pace of technological change, look no further than *Megatrends 2000*.[9] As the millennium approached, John Naisbitt and Patricia Aburdene set about predicting the future shape of the global economy. One word was conspicuous by its absence in their study: the internet. Even as late as 1990, no one anticipated the explosive impact of information technology. Bill Clinton said that when he became President of the United States in 1993 there were 50 registered websites. By the time he left office eight years later, there were over 350 million.

We live in a digital age. Today the internet provides access to rafts of knowledge. I find the world of instant communication and information exchange hugely exciting, but having access to more information does not necessarily mean I am a wiser person. T. S. Eliot's lament in 'Choruses from "The Rock"' continues to sound a warning note as it did when it was published in 1934:

> Where is the life we have lost in living?
> Where is the wisdom we have lost in knowledge?
> Where is the knowledge we have lost in information?[10]

Eliot is right to challenge us. Life is about more than the accumulation of information – as is education. It is why the Latin (western) tradition distinguishes *sapientia* (wisdom) from *scientia* – the word from which we get our word 'science', meaning knowledge. The Greek (eastern) tradition makes a similar distinction between *sophia* (wisdom) and *gnosis* (knowledge). The Christian tradition is united in insisting that we need wisdom to live well and to negotiate change, and wisdom is not what we know *about* but what we *intuitively* know, the distillation of experience and reflection. In our anxiety and bewilderment, we need discernment, which, in Christian understanding, comes only from God. We need soul food for the journey.

Signs of an environmental catastrophe

Jesus may have praised his contemporaries for their ability to interpret changes in the weather, but our generation has been reluctant to face up to mounting evidence of global warming and climate change in unseasonal and extreme weather patterns. We have been wilfully indifferent to the warnings of environmental scientists. Pictures of oceans clogged with discarded plastic, the degradation of productive farmland because of drought, rising sea levels and the catastrophic decline of biodiversity in some parts of the world have finally succeeded in introducing an urgency into public and private discourse. We have woken up to the scale of the crisis. Some say it is the defining challenge of our generation. Across the world people are using the language of climate emergency and environmental catastrophe to express a mixture of anguish, frustration and anger. There remain a few 'climate change deniers' but they are outliers in the scientific community and in the global conversation about how best to care for the planet.

An era of fake news

What is truth? It was Pilate who famously asked the question of Jesus at his trial. His question continues to have traction because two new terms have entered the English lexicon: 'post-truth' and 'fake news'. The *Oxford English Dictionary* defines 'post-truth' as 'relating to or denoting circumstances in which objective facts are less influential in shaping public opinion than appeals to emotion and personal belief'. In George Orwell's prophetic novel *Nineteen Eighty-Four*, the 'Ministry of Truth' controls the corporate memory of society by continuously editing history to ensure that there is no memory of a time when Big Brother was not right. Orwell realizes that if you can control people's memories you can control their capacity to imagine a different future. It is why the teaching of history is ultimately a moral issue. Revisionist historians are still busy trying to convince us that the Holocaust never happened. In China there were riots following the publication of Japanese textbooks that gave scant acknowledgement of the atrocities committed by the Imperial Japanese Army on mainland China during World War Two. Selective amnesia has global ramifications because it distorts the past and promotes inaccurate remedies to international problems. In an era of fake news and malign postings on social media, how do we know what is true?

Orwell imagines a terrifying world of endless war and universal surveillance. He invents terms like 'newspeak' and 'doublethink'. He gives slogans to dictators: Black is White, War is Peace, Freedom is Slavery, Ignorance is Strength. Writing in 1946 in an essay titled 'Politics and the English Language', he argues that 'political chaos is connected with the decay of language'. 'If thought corrupts language,' he says, 'language can also corrupt thought.' Unregulated free speech can be dangerous, but regulation does not equate to the freedom not to be offended. Free speech does not give the green light to the aggressive use of social media to intimidate others or the 'no platforming' of speakers on university campuses. A 'cancel culture' that tries to keep opposing views from being heard is bad news. Freedom of speech may not be an absolute, but it is a touchstone of a free society.

In our post-truth world, what is profoundly disturbing is not only people's lack of awareness but their seeming indifference to the lies they are being told. In the 1930s, Nazi propaganda succeeded in propagating lies and hatred of the Jews with devastating efficiency. Thanks to the reach of digital platforms, fake news is a burgeoning industry. Assaults on truth and the abuse of free speech constitute major threats to democratic institutions and the maintenance of trust in the concept of 'society'. We should not be surprised at the widespread cynicism infecting western society. It takes root in soil poisoned by lies and cover-ups, particularly when those in positions of public trust are discovered to have been 'economical with the truth'.[11] The indifference of unaccountable power and a callous propensity to close ranks are yet more symptoms of the problem.[12]

In the quest for truth, the manipulation of images and voices is introducing a further level of complexity. How can we be sure that this statement, this voice, this photograph is authentic? According to the famous saying, 'A lie travels halfway round the world before the truth has put its boots on'. If that was the case in days gone by, how much more so today in the world of instantaneous communication? Trust is in short supply when you can be easily hoodwinked. In a fog of misinformation, it is easy to lose confidence in the very notion of truth. You tell me your truth and I will tell you mine. All perceptions of truth are partial and to an extent provisional, including those of Christians, but this does not mean that we should not evaluate competing claims to truth. The idea that everything is true or equally worthwhile is illusory.

The London School of Economics (LSE) identifies what it terms 'Five Giant Evils' affecting western society: confusion, cynicism, fragmentation, irresponsibility and apathy, each of which it says must be challenged lest the fabric of western civilization is undermined irretrievably.[13] To their list I would add tribalism. The startling apocalyptic language of the LSE analysis echoes the language of spiritual warfare used by St Paul in his letters.[14] If their analysis is correct, then there is no single remedy to our current malaise. That should not signal despair, but it should prompt a deeper search for wisdom and a desire to collaborate across political and cultural divides for the sake of the common good.

The Church has considerable convening power and experience in building coalitions of goodwill, which is why it should never be a closed space that needs to be defended. Rather, through its network of churches, chaplaincies and schools, it should seek to offer hospitality and welcome, safe spaces and 'human-sized' communities for those concerned about a loss of identity and social cohesion. The Church has a part to play in the search for wisdom, provided it enters conversations with imagination and humility, and a spiritual disposition to listen. After all, Christianity does not have all the answers. The full purpose of life is not known and is perhaps unknowable. In this life, 'we see through a glass darkly'.[15] 'What we will be has not yet been revealed', says St John.[16] Being a Christian is about living in the provisional – in St Paul's language, 'walking by faith' – and that means living with potentially unanswerable questions as we grapple with the 'signs of our times'. With our neighbours of all faiths and none, we need to reflect on the ordinary, sad, tragic and funny events of our lives, and identify wholesome values by which to live. We cannot afford to opt out and abdicate responsibility for translating our private experiences into the public realm we share and create.

In pursuit of happiness

Shopping for bargains in the sales, I encountered a stand promoting New Year resolutions. Customers entering the shop were offered five different leaflets: 'Feel healthier', 'Feel happier', 'Lose weight', 'Stop smoking', 'Look great'. There were plenty of copies of each handout except one: the leaflets entitled 'Feel happier' had all been taken. Pleasure can be measured. So can things that cause us to be miserable or fearful or to go to the doctor, and it has provoked an avalanche of publications from academic studies to self-help books.

According to Thomas Jefferson and the American Declaration of Independence,[17] certain truths are self-evident; namely, 'All men are created equal, that they are endowed by their Creator with certain unalienable Rights, that among these are Life, Liberty and the pursuit of Happiness'. Jefferson drew upon the teaching of the Scottish philosopher John Locke[18] and, in his memoirs, explains how his life had been directed towards creating 'an opening for the aristocracy of virtue and talent' with which to replace the old aristocracy of wealth and privilege. For both Jefferson and Locke, 'the pursuit of happiness' meant not hedonism but living a virtuous life. People must direct their energies to worthwhile ends.

What constitutes happiness is always interesting to debate. The American Declaration of Independence speaks about the right to pursue happiness, not the right to happiness *per se*. With the passing of the years, the subtlety of this distinction has become obscured, with the result that happiness is now seen as an entitlement. Shorn of its altruism, Jefferson's statement has been erected into the manifesto of the western world, generating massive and unrealistic expectations. Happiness is my birthright: if I'm not happy, then somebody must be to blame.

The reality is that there have always been those who are unhappy because they are disturbed, whose fear and anxiety are pathological, and who become ill or trapped in addictive or compulsive behaviours. What is a new and worrying trend, however, is the level of stress-related illness and breakdown among children and young people.[19] Self-harming has reached epic proportions, in part fuelled by social media. What has gone wrong that our children should feel that this is the only way they can communicate or ask for help? What distorted images of themselves are they living with?

Jonathan Haidt, Social Psychologist and Professor of Ethical Leadership at New York University, says: 'Anxiety and its associated disorders seem to be the defining mental illnesses of young people today.'[20] In his book *The Anxious Generation*, he argues that the decline of free play in childhood and the rise of smartphone usage among adolescents are the twin sources of increased mental distress among teenagers. 'There has been a historic and unprecedented transformation of human childhood',[21] and what he calls the 'Great Rewiring' of adolescents' brains, triggered by various technological developments: the availability of smartphones with apps, the installation of front-facing cameras on smartphones which enable people to take selfies, the ability to repost and retweet, and the development of algorithms that foster dependency. He says that once young people began carrying the entire internet in their pockets, available to them day and night, it altered their daily experiences and developmental pathways.

Meanwhile, absenteeism is a growing phenomenon among young professionals. Time off work for stress is the highest it has ever been. Young professionals are naturally ambitious and may have higher expectations than earlier generations, but this does not explain why one in five are on some form of tranquillizer or anti-depressant. Companies and financial institutions are willing to pay their employees ludicrous salaries in return for unrestricted working hours, but it puts increased pressure on health and family life. Alain de Botton has coined the term 'status anxiety' to describe the pressure that young working people experience, which he says underlies these disturbing statistics. He identifies its chief causes as job insecurity, pressure at work to perform, the need to earn enough money, and anxiety about health.[22]

Choice and self-realization

In the pursuit of happiness, choice has become the mantra of the political classes. Increased choice, it is argued, leads to an increase in happiness, though with scant evidence to support the claim. Supermarket shelves groan with foods from around the world, brochures offer wondrous holidays, and phone companies compete to offer cheap deals. Some choices are trivial, but some will determine the direction of our lives. In a voyeuristic age, what the explosion of choice has succeeded in doing is to introduce yet another level of anxiety.[23] The desire for a smarter car, a Rolex watch or an exotic holiday can push us to overwork and we become ill.

Not everyone is excited by a plethora of options. Intimidated by the complexity of the choices before them, some doubt their ability to make good decisions and end up demoralized. Demoralization has always had a double sense in English: it indicates both a loss of moral meaning *and* a loss of hope. At times in life it can be a question of choosing the least bad option. Psychologists call this spiral of discontent and unhappiness 'consumer vertigo'.[24] It is a modern version of a question the prophet Isaiah asked centuries ago: 'Why do you waste your money on that which is not bread and your labour on that which fails to satisfy?'[25] In moments of dissatisfaction or unbridled envy, we might ask ourselves the same question. Contrary to the sales pitches that daily bombard me, I am not empowered by being given more and more options. I am empowered when I discover values with which to make good decisions. To exalt individual choice and self-realization puts an unhealthy focus on what I can get for myself and undervalues what I can contribute to others and the common good.

The loss of transcendence

In an interview shortly before he died, the poet Seamus Heaney said, 'The biggest change in my lifetime has been the evaporation of the transcendent from public discourse.' In Heaney's view, our generation is so enmeshed in the immediacy of short-term transactional language, buying and selling, exchanging information, exploring options, that we find it embarrassing and/or difficult to discuss the mysterious dimensions of life, the things that speak of God and eternity. There is no doubt that a climate of negativity and suspicion surrounds religion in Britain today. For many people religious language has lost its traction. Critics delight in casting faith in opposition to the enlightened forces of science and egalitarianism that form the secular heartbeat. It has become fashionable to portray religion as the handmaid of ignorance. In the minds of some, science has dethroned God and become the infallible arbiter of truth. For Heaney, faith is not in opposition to science: faith enriches our understanding of life, placing it on a surer foundation and in an eternal perspective. It is why he laments cultural sterility and the 'evaporation' of the transcendent from public discourse.

In western liberal democracies, practically everything is permitted but practically nothing is forgiven. Society is heavy with accusation, as is evident from the way politicians regularly abuse, defame and discredit one another. Politics is necessarily adversarial, but the language of hatred and open contempt evident in some politicians' speeches is toxic. Punch and Judy politics whips up tension and polarizes public opinion. It does not build consensus or foster a culture of mutual respect and collaboration. Social media encourages us to make quick judgements with little concern for the wellbeing of those we criticize and scant knowledge of the context in which they live, act and speak. And, of course, social media forgets nothing. A single mistake, a misplaced tweet, a moment of madness, will stay on your record for ever. Typically, the liturgy of public discourse begins 'I accuse', rarely 'I confess'. Apologies are demanded but with little prospect of forgiveness.

Today's world is divided into victims and perpetrators. Any association with the wrongdoing of your ancestors taints you. Former heroes are trashed overnight as villains; statues torn down; schools, buildings and roads renamed; cherished family and cultural heritage is ridiculed. Revisiting our colonial history is a welcome step in the search for national integrity, but contested history needs interpretation, not eradication. George Orwell did not champion corporate amnesia. And here is the challenge. How do we speak into our angry, shouty world of accusation and counter-accusation, where people seem keener to point the finger and apportion blame than to listen and work for the common good? Jesus replaces the politics of ritual and racial purity with the politics of compassion, but our generation seems trapped in a purity contest. People work hard to disassociate themselves from the impure, from those who are different or think differently. How do we recover the language of grace, the language of justice with forgiveness, in a generation that applauds the untainted and uncontaminated?

The search for meaning

Although the transcendent may have evaporated from public discourse, there is a seam of cultural restlessness that warrants exploration. North American and European society has moved away from the perceived constraints of religion, tradition and ritual, and become more secular and anonymous. Today when seeking advice, we turn more readily to a doctor, personal trainer or therapist than a priest. We prefer to stay at home and watch the television than attend church, but the search for community, meaning and happiness remain strong. We have a seemingly insatiable appetite for anything that may contribute to our well-being. We mistrust dogma and are reluctant to use religious language but crave the ether of spirituality without being sure what it is. We are more interested in how something feels than whether it is true. Does it work for you?

The word 'religion' has its origin in the Latin verb 'to bind together': religion binds us to God and to one another. This is why, in the Judaeo-Christian tradition, spirituality is more than a lifestyle choice on a par with a subscription to the gym. The teaching of Jesus is that the goal of human striving is self-transcendence, not self-obsession. And here lies a further challenge for the Church today: theology must be relational, not a compendium of abstract truths. Spirituality and worship must reconnect with the realities of daily life and the lived wisdom of people, with the world as it actually is.

'They are to do good, to be rich in good works, generous, and ready to share, thus storing up for themselves the treasure of a good foundation for the future, so that they may take hold of the life that really is life.'[26] The words, attributed to St Paul, point to an understanding of spirituality as 'aliveness'. For the Christian, such aliveness will be rooted in prayer and shaped by the values of God's kingdom. It will be hallmarked by the cross, the mark of our shared baptism into Christ's saving death and resurrection. Authentic spirituality is about the action of God in the world and the life of grace within us; it is about the personal transformation that comes from being radically open to the Holy Spirit. 'I came that [you] may have life, and have it abundantly,'[27] says Jesus, or, as some translations have it, 'that you may have life in all its fullness'. Jesus promises a quality of life discovered through repentance, forgiveness, service and costly self-giving love. In the words of the Psalmist, it is a quality of life infused with the joy of knowing that 'goodness and mercy shall follow me all the days of my life'.[28] So how do we thrive, not just survive, in this second 'Age of Anxiety'?

Managing our anxiety

Thomas Merton, Trappist monk and one of the great spiritual writers of the twentieth century, says that anxiety is something we impose on ourselves and on one another: 'Ours is a time of anxiety because we have willed it to be so. Our anxiety is not imposed on us by force from outside. We impose it on our world and upon one another from within ourselves.'[29] I hear myself speak and see myself act as if being busy is a force outside my control. I get anxious, put myself under pressure and distribute my angst among my friends, family and colleagues. Busy, of course, is relative. There is being busy and feeling too busy. Either way, the responsibility is mine. I choose to live like this. Or to think I live like this. If I fuel my stress by the way I live, no amount of medication will help.

The daily challenge is to live without anxiety in the midst of it. Part of the solution lies in accurately diagnosing and addressing the roots of our anxiety and fear. We need to marshal resources to build resilience and cultivate an authentic spirituality. We need to slow down and strive for a better balance in our life. There is a frantic side to modern living that we need actively to resist, and this is where traditional spiritual practices, rooted in a rule of life, can help. Taking time to pray and meditate, to be still and to reflect, is fundamental. So is thanksgiving. When thanksgiving becomes a personal discipline, it unlocks the imagination and stirs us to be generous with our time, attention and money. We need to be thankful for what we have and not become obsessed about what we don't have or what the adverts tell us we ought to have. When we acknowledge life as a gift from God, we become less self-centred and more willing to share the good things of this world with others. These are themes that we will explore in the course of this book. Anxiety shrinks us. Thanksgiving and serving others expand us. We become bigger people.

Billy Connolly, the Scottish comedian and raconteur, says that there is no such thing as bad weather, only the wrong clothes. Perhaps it is time for we Christians to stop complaining about the bad weather, saying things are against us in our secular culture, and instead find the right clothes and the right ways of living in it and speaking into it? How can we read the 'signs of our times' in the light of the gospel and engage with our contemporaries in the places where they live and work so that they too can 'take hold of the life that really is life'?

In our efforts to recover a more holistic way of living and to live into the promises of the gospel, we could do worse than take the advice of the prophet Jeremiah: 'Stand at the crossroads, and look, and ask for the ancient paths, where the good way lies; and walk in it, and find rest for your souls.'[30] Given that, in company with many of our generation, we respond more readily to stories than to abstract propositions, the story of Jonah can come to our aid. As we stand bewildered at the crossroads, wondering which path to take, we turn to Jonah, who is the guide and spiritual companion for times such as these.

Reflections

- Which of the 'signs of the times' most concern you?

- During periods of change and uncertainty, what things help you to be resilient?

- 'Cast all your anxieties on God, for God cares about you' (1 Peter 5.7). What are the roots of anxiety and fear in your life? What anxieties or concerns do you *not* pray about or share with others but hug to yourself?

- Are you carrying burdens that others could help you with?

- Do you know someone going through difficulty whom you could support?

- Make a list of things for which you are thankful and consciously bring them into your daily prayers.

>   Deliver us, Lord, from every evil
>   and grant us peace in our day.
>   In your mercy, keep us free from sin
>   and protect us from all anxiety
>   as we wait in joyful hope
>   for the coming of our Saviour, Jesus Christ.

I fled Him, down the
   nights and down the
   days;
I fled Him, down the
   arches of the years;
I fled Him, down the
   labyrinthine ways
Of my own mind; and
   in the mist of tears
I hid from Him, and
   under running
   laughter.
Up vistaed hopes
   I sped;
And shot, precipitated,
Adown Titanic glooms of chasmèd fears,
From those strong Feet that followed, followed after.
But with unhurrying chase,
And unperturbèd pace,
Deliberate speed, majestic instancy,
They beat – and a Voice beat
More instant than the Feet –
'All things betray thee, who betrayest me.'

Francis Thompson (1859–1907)
'The Hound of Heaven'

2
The reluctant prophet

Let me begin by nailing my colours to the mast. I do not think that the Book of Jonah should be interpreted literally. Aside from the obvious biological question of whether a human being could remain alive in the belly of a fish for three days, a literal interpretation of the book raises various theological and historical problems. First, what sort of God causes a storm and suffering to innocent people in order to preserve the life of an individual, this man called Jonah? And, to be frank, would you want to trust such a God? Second, why did the later prophets who prophesied against Assyria know nothing of the extraordinary repentance of the people of Nineveh, to which, in another generation, Jesus referred regularly and approvingly?

Scholars debate these questions endlessly. There is a reference to Jonah the Prophet, the son of Amittai, in 2 Kings 14.25. He appears to have been active in the northern kingdom of Israel during the reign of Jeroboam II, but the consensus of biblical scholars is that, aside from the name, he has nothing to do with the Book of Jonah. Some call the book, confusingly to my mind, a Jewish novel[31] and others an extended prose poem. In all probability, it is a fictional story about one man's wrestling with God as he searches for purpose and meaning in his life. As such, it belongs to the same genre of literature as other 'fictional stories' in the Bible such as the Book of Job, which explores the problem of innocent suffering. The Book of Jonah is, to adopt Paul Murray's phrase, a study in the spirituality of bewilderment.

The book operates on two levels. At the human level, it explores Jonah's relationship with God and his struggle to understand that God's love has no limits. At a theological level, it is a searing critique of the complacent and patronizing attitude his contemporaries exhibited to neighbouring nations following their return from exile. The book pushes the envelope of Jewish understanding of God's good purposes and opens a window on to the Gentile world. As Martin Luther observed, the Book of Jonah is 'a wonderful sign of God's goodness to all the world'.[32] In our environmentally conscious days, I would go further and say that it is a wonderful sign of God's concern for all creation.

Date and background

Unlike the other prophetic books in the Hebrew Bible, nowhere does this book claim to be written by Jonah. Instead, it is a story *about* a man called Jonah, a meditation on the cost of being a prophet in the service of the God of Israel. Except where stated, the translation I use is the *New Revised Standard Version*; however, when quoting from the psalms I use the Psalter in *Common Worship*. Wherever it says 'God', it is translating the Hebrew *'elohim*. When it uses small capital letters, 'the LORD', in English, it is translating the Hebrew name for the God of Israel,[33] which may be transliterated as YHWH. In some English translations this is rendered as Yahweh, and in older translations as Jehovah. In

Jewish thought the sacred name was considered too holy ever to be spoken. As we shall see, the translators' convention is helpful because there are insights in the Hebrew text which might otherwise pass the casual reader by.

The date of the book is judged to be post-exilic – in other words, *after* the return of thousands of Jews from exile in Babylon, but *before* the rise of Alexander the Great. We know this because the focus of the book, as Jesus himself was aware, is Nineveh, the capital of the neo-Assyrian Empire. The forced detention and deportation of Jews by the Assyrians began in 722 BCE, following their successful invasion of the northern kingdom of Israel. Nineveh was the largest city in the world and remained so until 612 BCE, when, after a bitter civil war, it was sacked by a coalition of its former subject peoples: the Medes from north of Persia and the Chaldeans from southern Babylonia. The city was never rebuilt. The Assyrian Empire had already begun to fall apart following the death of its great leader Asshurbanipal in 627 BCE and when the hated Nineveh was sacked and destroyed by invading armies, Assyrian control of the Near East came to an end.

The Assyrians had dominated Mesopotamia and the eastern Mediterranean for centuries. Although their empire collapsed, their organization survived and served as a template for the new Chaldean Empire that took its place. Babylon rose to fresh prominence. Its armies succeeded in defeating neighbouring kingdoms and, following a successful invasion of the southern kingdom of Judah and the capture of Jerusalem, they initiated further deportations between 597 BCE and 587 BCE in response to Jewish uprisings. It is estimated that upwards of 10,000

Jews were deported.[34] Unlike earlier deportations, only the most prominent citizens of Judah were forced to relocate to Babylon: men and women from the professional classes, priests, scribes, craftspeople and the wealthy. The so-called 'people of the land', *'am ha'aretz*, were allowed to remain. The exile ended in 538 BCE, when the Chaldeans were themselves overthrown by the Persians under Cyrus the Great, who allowed the Jews to return home. The Persian Empire was to survive a further 200 years, until it too was conquered by Alexander the Great in 330 BCE and subsumed into his vast Greek Empire.

Some scholars argue that the Book of Jonah was written in the post-exilic period because of the presence of Aramaisms[35] in the Hebrew text. Others argue for an earlier date – in the seventh or eighth century BCE. The date of the book, however, is less important than its message. The exile was a major crisis for the Jews, just as their enslavement in Egypt had been for their forebears centuries earlier. Why had this tragedy happened? Jewish self-understanding was built on the premise that God would protect his chosen people and use them for his good purposes in the world. The collapse first of the northern kingdom of Israel and then of the southern kingdom of Judah, and above all the sack and destruction of the Temple in Jerusalem and the taking of their Davidic king as prisoner,[36] implied that their faith in the promises of Yahweh was misplaced. Had God abandoned his people?

With the overthrow of the Chaldeans, the accession of King Cyrus and the return of the exiles from Babylon, a new self-confidence surges in the Jewish people. Jerusalem and its Temple are rebuilt. God had not deserted them. But the return from exile also spawns a resurgent and arrogant nationalism, and this is the backdrop to the story of Jonah. The book was almost certainly written with these returning exiles in mind, for whom the destruction of Nineveh was old news, but the future of a restored Judah was uncertain. It seems to have been written as a counterblast to the smugness and exclusivity that was emerging in the restored Jewish community. As such, it is less a historical record of the work of the prophet Jonah than a parable about the danger of insularity. God's purposes are great. God loves all people and acts to redeem all nations, not just Israel.

The call of Jonah

> Now the word of the LORD came to Jonah, son of Amittai, saying, 'Go at once to Nineveh, that great city, and cry out against it; for their wickedness has come up before me.' But Jonah set out to flee to Tarshish from the presence of the LORD. He went down to Joppa and found a ship going to Tarshish; so he paid his fare and went on board, to go with them to Tarshish, away from the presence of the LORD.[37]

Wake up! There is an immediacy about the Book of Jonah. Be open to God. Change. The call to repentance and the urgency with which it is to be delivered is evident from the outset. Yahweh is not only Israel's God; he is Lord of the whole world. Yahweh is interested not simply in the Jewish people, but in every nation on earth. God observes and will move against sin, corruption and injustice anywhere on the globe because God's loving concern embraces women and men everywhere. But why Nineveh?

Why Nineveh?

In pre-exilic times, the Assyrians were seen as the bitterest enemies of the people of Israel, and their capital occupied an iconic place in Jewish imagination. Nineveh was hated, as we see in the book of the prophet Nahum. Written in all probability shortly after the city's fall, Nahum is unremitting in his denunciation of the cruelty and immorality of the people of Nineveh.[38] He trumpets its destruction as good news, confirmation of the goodness of God towards his own people.[39]

Nineveh is situated in what is today Iraq. It was built on a tell on the eastern bank of the Tigris, near a natural crossing of the river, on the foundations of a more ancient city constructed by the Babylonians. On the opposite bank stands the modern city of Mosul. Sennacherib acceded to the Assyrian throne in 705 BCE upon the death of his father, Sargon II, and ruled until his own death in 681 BCE. He was the second king of the Sargonid dynasty and the most powerful of the Assyrian kings, famous for his brutal military campaigns in the Middle East, his destruction of the city of Babylon in 689 BCE and his fortification of Nineveh. Scenes carved around 645 BCE on the wall of one of its palaces depict a magnificent city surrounded by turreted and crenellated walls.[40]

In modern times Nineveh was excavated by the British Archaeological Survey. Following World War One and the collapse of the Ottoman Empire, the world map was carved up by the victorious powers and new countries and protectorates were created. Mesopotamia (as it was then called) came to Britain. Trustees of the British Museum, anxious to protect antiquities from plunder, successfully negotiated for Reginald Campbell Thompson, a former assistant in the museum and serving in the British army in the region, to be attached to the British expeditionary force. He investigated Ur and various ancient sites, and in 1931 invited fellow archaeologist Max Mallowan and his wife Agatha Christie to assist in the excavation of Nineveh. Anyone who has visited Agatha Christie's home at Greenway on the banks of the River Dart in Devon, now owned by the National Trust, will have seen photographs and plans of the dig at Nineveh, together with various artefacts and mementos. Years later, Agatha Christie's time in Mesopotamia would provide her with material for her crime thriller *They Came to Baghdad.*

The pioneering work of the British Archaeological Survey was succeeded by an international team of archaeologists and scholars, among them Dr Thelma Akrawi, who fled to England with her husband and family as refugees from the rule of Saddam Hussein. By happy coincidence, the family (who were Syrian Orthodox Christians of the Antiochene Patriarchate) settled in my parish in north London and Dr Akrawi was able to provide me with a wealth of information about the dimensions and significance of the city.

In choosing to focus on the people of Nineveh, the unknown author of our story is making a strong statement to his contemporaries. He is saying: look, even those cruel Assyrians whom you despise are the object of Yahweh's care and compassion. In times of insecurity, it is always tempting to turn inwards, to pull up the drawbridge and man the barricades. We adopt a siege mentality and become mouthpieces of a tribal god. Like Jonah, we lose sight of God's call to take the good news of his love and compassion to all the world – just as Israel had lost sight of its role to bring the knowledge of the one true God to the ends of the earth. They had become a religious club, focused on their survival and membership – who was in and who was out – preoccupied with rules and regulations, not the world they were summoned to serve. The story of Jonah is a critique of their spiritual myopia.

Why Tarshish?

An atlas of the ancient world shows that Nineveh lay due east of Israel. But no sooner had Jonah received his commission than he 'set out to flee to Tarshish to escape from the presence of the LORD. He went down to Joppa and found a ship bound for Tarshish'. Tarshish was an ancient Semitic colony on the far side of the Mediterranean, on the coast of south-west Spain near modern-day Cadiz. It was on the edge of the known world. The region was famous for its extensive mineral deposits, as a result of which Tarshish had grown into a trading centre of international significance. In other words, God instructs Jonah to go east to Iraq, but Jonah is terrified and goes west to Spain. He sails to Spain in the belief that there he will be beyond the jurisdiction and reach of Yahweh, the God of Israel. He can escape God.

The futility of Jonah's flight may have provided Francis Thompson with the inspiration for his poem 'The Hound of Heaven' (see in more detail on p. 20):

> I fled Him, down the nights and down the days;
> I fled Him, down the arches of the years;
> I fled Him, down the labyrinthine ways
> Of my own mind.[41]

It certainly finds an echo in Psalm 139, one of the most moving and deeply personal psalms in the Psalter, which could be read as a commentary on the attempted flight of Jonah:

> O LORD, you have searched me out and known me.
> You mark out my journeys and my resting places,
> and are acquainted with all my ways.
> You encompass me behind and before and lay your hand
>   upon me.
> Where can I go then from your spirit? Where can I flee
>   from your presence?
> If I climb up into heaven, you are there.
> If I make the grave my bed, you are there also.
> If I take the wings of the morning
> and dwell at the uttermost limits of the sea,
> even there your hand shall lead me and your right hand
>   shall hold me fast.[42]

Jonah attempts to escape the God of Israel by travelling 'to the uttermost limits of the sea'. He fails. 'Who can hide in secret places so that I cannot see them? says the LORD. Do I not fill heaven and earth? says the LORD,'[43] words recorded by the prophet Jeremiah. Like Jeremiah and the Psalmist, Jonah discovers that he cannot escape the Almighty, and this knowledge deepens his relationship with God. A key word in Psalm 139 is the verb 'to know', *yadah*. It occurs no less than six times and each time God is the subject of the verb, emphasizing God's omniscience and omnipresence. We know and are known by God. Centuries later, St Paul will expand on this idea when writing his great 'Hymn to Love' in his First Letter to the Corinthians: 'For now we see in a mirror, dimly, but then we will see face to face. Now I know only in part; then I will know fully, even as I have been fully known.'[44]

Our longing for God is a response to the God who is searching for us, a search that will find fulfilment on the last day when we see God 'face to face'. The Scriptures speak of an intimacy with God which is transformative but never cosy. The deepening of our understanding of God often comes as a surprise. The experience is variously described as an encounter, a meeting or a conversation. Whichever metaphor is chosen, it is always something that God initiates. Prayer is something that God does in us. Our part is to open ourselves to God in love and trust. God is not to be annexed to a drive for self-improvement. The purpose of prayer is to make us available to God – not the other way round. This is something Jonah discovers painfully and dramatically when a storm threatens to capsize the ship.

The storm

> But the LORD hurled a great wind upon the sea, and such a mighty storm came upon the sea that the ship threatened to break up. Then the mariners were afraid, and each cried to his god. They threw the cargo that was in the ship into the sea, to lighten it for them. Jonah, meanwhile, had gone down into the hold of the ship and had lain down, and was fast asleep. The captain came and said to him, 'What are you doing sound asleep? Get up, call on your god! Perhaps the god will spare us a thought so that we do not perish.'
>
> The sailors said to one another, 'Come, let us cast lots, so that we may know on whose account this calamity has

come upon us.' So they cast lots, and the lot fell on Jonah. Then they said to him, 'Tell us why this calamity has come upon us. What is your occupation? Where do you come from? What is your country? And of what people are you?' 'I am a Hebrew,' he replied. 'I worship the LORD, the God of heaven, who made the sea and the dry land.' Then the men were even more afraid, and said to him, 'What is this that you have done!' For the men knew that he was fleeing from the presence of the LORD, because he had told them so.

Then they said to him, 'What shall we do to you, that the sea may quieten down for us?' For the sea was growing more and more tempestuous. He said to them, 'Pick me up and throw me into the sea; then the sea will quieten down for you; for I know it is because of me that this great storm has come upon you.' Nevertheless, the men rowed hard to bring the ship back to land, but they could not, for the sea grew more and more stormy against them. Then they cried out to the LORD, 'Please, O LORD, we pray, do not let us perish on account of this man's life. Do not make us guilty of innocent blood; for you, O LORD, have done as it pleased you.' So they picked Jonah up and threw him into the sea; and the sea ceased from its raging. Then the men feared the LORD even more, and they offered a sacrifice to the LORD and made vows. But the LORD provided a large fish to swallow up Jonah; and Jonah was in the belly of the fish for three days and three nights.[45]

'What are you doing?' shouts the terrified captain at Jonah. Despite the ferocity of the storm, Jonah is fast asleep in the hold of the ship. 'Get up, and call on your god. Perhaps the god will spare us so that we do not perish.' For Christians, the incident has an immediate resonance with the story about the storm on the lake in Galilee, with Jesus fast asleep at the back of the boat, his head on a cushion.[46] There too the petrified disciples wake him up and beg for his help: 'Lord, save us! Do you not care that we are perishing?' Unlike Jonah who suffers the indignity of being thrown overboard, Jesus calms the storm with a word. No wonder Jesus's disciples are unsure about what sort of man this is that 'even the winds and the sea obey him.' The contrast illustrates another aspect to 'the sign of Jonah' to which Jesus refers. Something greater than Jonah is here because, unlike our recalcitrant prophet who ends up getting thrown overboard, Jesus exercises divine power over the wind and waves.

The Hebrew verb *qum*, used to summon Jonah out of his lethargy, is also used in the Book of Genesis by God when addressing Abram as he begins his journey to Canaan. The same verb is used in Isaiah 60 to express the vocation of God's people. 'Arise, shine; for your light has come, and the glory of the LORD has risen upon you.' In each case, God summons us to get up and get going. What is striking about the text in Jonah is that it is the captain of the ship, a foreigner, who speaks with the voice of Yahweh to Jonah. We should not be surprised when God speaks to us through strangers, including those of other faiths and none. One of the temptations of social media is to follow only those with whom we agree or are in sympathy with. Mentally we 'no platform' those with whom we disagree and reduce our chance of being challenged, of hearing something new, a voice from outside our comfort-zone, and perhaps the voice of God.

The point is reinforced by the crew's interrogation of Jonah. 'Why has this calamity overtaken us?' they ask. 'What is your occupation? Where do you come from? What is your country? Of what people are you?' And Jonah answers, 'I am a Hebrew, and I worship the LORD, the God of heaven, who made the sea and the dry land.' 'The God of heaven' was a common Persian title for the God of the Jews. The title is found on the so-called 'Cyrus Cylinder', now in the care of the British Museum. It is also used in King Cyrus's royal injunction to the people of his empire, quoted in the books of Ezra and Nehemiah, instructing them to provide resources for the Jews returning from exile in Babylon to the land of Judah so that they can rebuild the Temple in Jerusalem.

What is noteworthy here is that Jonah now specifically declares God to have made *the sea* as well as the land. Jonah has learned that, even if he were to attempt to travel to the 'uttermost limits of the sea', he cannot escape God. God is not to be defined by human constructs or confined by national borders. Jonah has learned through bitter experience what previously he had known only intellectually. It is sometimes said that the longest journey is the journey from the mind to the heart. Theophan the Recluse (1815-94), one of the great teachers of prayer in the Russian Orthodox Church, says, 'The principal thing [about prayer] is to stand with your mind in your heart before God, and to go on standing before God unceasingly day and night until the end of your life.'[47] Prayer is a *via integrata*: a journey into the wholeness that God desires for each of us.

'Not all those who wander are lost'

Devotees of J. R. R. Tolkein's epic *The Lord of the Rings* will immediately recognize the words of Bilbo Baggins in his poem 'The Riddle of Strider', written in honour of Aragorn and referring to his travels and destiny. Exploration and wandering can have purpose and meaning even if this is not apparent, at least not at first. The truth is that not everyone who is searching or exploring is aimless. It is not without reason that, in a variety of literature and across different cultures, our inner world is often pictured as a landscape, the contours and pitfalls of which we can find ourselves navigating in times of personal crisis. The Jesuit poet Gerard Manley Hopkins coined the word 'inscape' to describe such experiences. In one of his so-called 'dark sonnets', he famously says: 'O the mind, mind has mountains; cliffs of fall frightful, sheer, no-man-fathomed.'[48] In Shakespeare's *King Lear*, many of Lear's awakenings occur in the chaos of a storm and the torrential downpour on the heath. The external phenomena reflect and symbolize his internal confusion. We are told that Lear experiences a 'tempest in the mind'.[49] In the same way, the storm that results in Jonah being thrown overboard is less a physical phenomenon than a description of an intense personal crisis.

This understanding is not a modern take on an ancient text. Earlier generations understood intuitively what was being communicated by the author of Jonah. For example, in an anonymous Latin Christian poem based on the story of Jonah, dated to the end of the second century and at one stage attributed to the north African theologian Tertullian (c.155–c.220 CE), Jonah cries out: 'In me is the storm. In me is all the madness of the world.'[50] In her study *Reading Genesis*, the American novelist Marilynne

Robinson explores the great biblical themes that underscore and illuminate what it is to be human. She makes this interesting observation about the way the Hebrew Scriptures attempt to communicate their wisdom: 'The Bible does not exist to explain away mysteries and complexities but to reveal and explore them with a respect and restraint that resists conclusion.'[51] Ambiguity does not always sit easily in the modern mind, used as we are to the supposed clarity of scientific discourse.

Psychologists tell us that the blurring of boundaries between fantasy and reality, issuing in chaos, is a salient feature in the experience of the neurotic or psychotic person. No one is free from the risk that our experience or behaviour might, under stress, become chaotic and destructive. Which is why the journey to personal integration requires not the repudiation and elimination of chaos, but a compromise with it. In contemporary usage, the word 'compromise' has a negative connotation, denoting moral shabbiness and lack of principle. But in relation to our inner world, compromise represents the mature fruit of the struggle for self-knowledge, the embrace and integration of difference.

Jonah realizes that his chaos is infecting and affecting others and asks to be thrown overboard. Reluctantly the crew do so and there is a great calm such that a 'great fear of Yahweh' descends on them. These foreigners come to a knowledge and worship of God *not* through Jonah's success, but through his abject failure. When life goes wrong, when we beat ourselves up over the bad choices we have made, when things fall apart and we are surrounded by the debris of relationships that have disintegrated, it is easy to despair. What the story of Jonah teaches me is that I should not underestimate the redemptive power of God to use such experiences for good. God can redeem my mistakes and failings and use them for his good purposes. Failure is not the end of the world. Losing God is. I take comfort in words spoken by God to the prophet Isaiah:

> But now thus says the LORD,
> he who created you, O Jacob, he who formed you, O Israel.
> Do not fear, for I have redeemed you.
> I have called you by name, you are mine.
> When you pass through the waters, I will be with you;
> and through the rivers, they shall not overwhelm you;
> when you walk through fire you shall not be burned,
> and the flame shall not consume you.
> For I am the LORD your God,
> the Holy One of Israel, your Saviour.[52]

We talk, sometimes in grandiose terms, about the quest for enlightenment, the search for meaning and purpose, the search for God. What this opening chapter of the Book of Jonah speaks of is not our search for God, but God's search for us. And, as Francis Thompson's poem declares, God pursues us relentlessly 'down the labyrinthine ways of my own mind'. In this context, it is interesting to note that in the New Testament, according to the fourth Gospel, the first recorded words of Jesus are not a statement but a question: 'What are you looking for?' (John 1.38). What do you seek? What is driving you? What do you want? 'Not all those who wander are lost' but, until we can answer this fundamental question of Jesus, our searching is likely to be no more than pirouetting on the surface and will end in frustration. The theme of God's search for us, for the least, the last and the lost, is recapitulated in many of Jesus's parables. Jesus talks of a father scanning the horizon for his prodigal son, of a widow searching frantically for a lost silver coin, of a shepherd roaming the hillsides in search of a missing sheep, of a merchant searching for the pearl of great price. Jonah's story of rebellion is equally poignant: God's saving purposes will not be thwarted by our sin, by our fear, by our mistakes and errors of judgement, by our failures or by our wilful disobedience. God will not let us go.

When I was a child, above the kitchen table hung an old sampler embroidered by my great-grandmother, with the closing verses of a poem. In truth, it was a bit of nineteenth-century doggerel, but its words fascinated me as a child and have accompanied me throughout my adult life:

> Man's life is laid in the loom of time
>   To a pattern he does not see,
> While the weavers work and the shuttles fly
>   Till the dawn of eternity.
>
> Some shuttles are filled with silver threads
>   And some with threads of gold,
> While often but the darker hues
>   Are all that they may hold.
>
> Not till the loom is silent,
>   And the shuttles cease to fly,
> Shall God reveal the pattern
>   And explain the reason why
>
> The dark threads were as needful
>   In the weaver's skilful hand
> As the threads of gold and silver
>   For the pattern which he planned.

Reflections

- Can you think of a time when you found yourself doing a task or a job you didn't want to do? What helped you cope?

- 'When you pass through the waters, I will be with you; and through rivers, they shall not overwhelm you.' Can you recall a time when this has been your experience? What did you learn from it?

- Looking back on your life, can you think of a way in which the hand of God has guided you?

Disturb us, O Lord,
when we are well pleased with ourselves,
when our dreams have come true because we have
 dreamed too little,
when we have arrived safely because we sailed too
 close to the shore.

Disturb us, O Lord,
when with the abundance of things we possess, we
 have lost our thirst for the waters of life;

when having fallen in love with life, we have ceased to
    dream of eternity;
when in our efforts to build a new earth, our vision of
    heaven has grown dim.

Disturb us, O Lord,
to venture on wider seas where storms will show us
    your mastery,
where losing sight of land, we shall discover the stars.
Expand the horizon of our hopes, we pray,
and launch us into your future
with strength, courage, hope and love.

>   Based on a prayer attributed to Sir Francis Drake that,
> it is claimed, he wrote and delivered to his crew in 1577
>   before sailing from Plymouth, England, on a
>   voyage of circumnavigation

I began the search for the meaning of life. At first, I was attracted by the pursuit of wealth and leisure. But, as most people discover, human nature wants something better to do than gourmandise and kill time. We have been given life in order to achieve something worthwhile, to make good use of our talents. It could not have been given us without some benefit in eternity. How otherwise could one regard as a gift from God a life which is painful, fraught with anxiety, which left to itself would simply wear out, from the prattle of the cradle to the drivel of senility? It is my belief that human beings, prompted by our very nature, have always sought to raise our sights through practice of the virtues such as patience, chastity and forgiveness, in the conviction that a good life is secured only through good deeds and good thoughts. Could the immortal God have given us life with no other horizon but death? Could the Giver of good inspire us with a sense of life only to have it overshadowed by a fear of death?

Hilary of Poitiers (c.310–c.367)
On the Trinity

3
The right road lost

'Midway on our life's journey, I found myself in dark woods, the right road lost'. With these words one of the greatest pieces of medieval literature begins, Dante's *Divine Comedy*. His words tallied with my own sense of bewilderment when, having spent ten years as a Benedictine monk, I left monastic life in middle age and 're-entered the world'. I remember arriving at Victoria underground station and discovering that in the intervening years London Transport had introduced a new ticket system. I stood next to a group of puzzled Japanese tourists and watched seasoned commuters effortlessly negotiating the new automatic barriers with their Oyster cards while I worked out what to do. A stranger in my own city, it was the first of many readjustments, part of a process of losing and finding. Dietrich Bonhoeffer's words in *The Cost of Discipleship* rang true:

> When Christ calls a person, he bids them come and die. It may be a death like that of the first disciples who had to leave home and work to follow him, or it may be a death like Luther's who had to leave the monastery and go out into the world, but it is the same death every time – death in Jesus Christ, the death of the old man at his call.[53]

I slept on the floor of my sister's flat in East London that night, contemplating an uncertain future and listening into the small hours to the Asian family next door celebrating their daughter's marriage. Barely 24 hours earlier I had sung compline with my community for the last time: 'Save us, O Lord, while waking, and guard us while sleeping.' Returning to my monastic cell, I had taken off my black Benedictine habit and hung it up on the back of the door as I had done every night for ten years. Opening the window, I breathed in lungsful of cool night air and listened to an owl hooting in the monastery woods. Now, lying on the floor, I felt I had exchanged Gregorian chant for Hindi music and firecrackers.

That first 24 hours was a bewildering experience. In the weeks that followed, I had to let go of a lot of things and come to terms with other things I had accepted intellectually but not emotionally. There was loss, the bereavement of losing the familiar, the cherished, the beautiful – and, hard as it may be to comprehend, monastic life is beautiful. There was loss of place, loss of friendships, people with whom I had shared the intimacies of life and death. There was anger. There was sadness. There was confusion. There was relief. I was uncertain where to look for seeds of hope for the future. Then I received an unexpected present. I recognized the handwriting on the jiffy bag but was puzzled by its contents: one cassette. A note inside said that it was what every ex-monk should listen to. I switched on the cassette player and heard the unmistakable voice of Gloria Gaynor singing 'I will survive', followed by M People singing 'Search for the hero inside yourself'. By the time I got to the happy-go-lucky whistling of Bobby McFerrin singing 'Don't worry, be happy', life seemed possible.

'Ask, and it will be given to you; search, and you will find; knock, and the door will be opened for you,' says Jesus.[54] Do not despair. The impetus to set out on your search is born out of a sense of loss and incompleteness: you recognize that something or someone is missing, that you are not where you want to be. It is why life is often described as a journey. For some, the journey is rich and colourful; for others, it is confusing and opaque, without direction, meaning or purpose. In my experience, life is more like a series of interlocking journeys: some with distinct beginnings and endings, others more diffuse and circuitous, some downright messy.

'And the end of all our exploring will be to arrive where we started and know the place for the first time.'[55] As one who does not find transitions in life easy, I find T. S. Eliot's words reassuring because he holds out the prospect not of endless futility, but of homecoming. Change can be hard whether it is leaving home, going to university, getting married or divorced, becoming a parent, moving house, moving into retirement, or leaving a monastery. Some transitions are visible, others hidden and more subtle. It may be some time before we recognize that something is going on that we need to attend to.

The mid-life crisis is well documented, though quite when it starts and ends is an open question. Mid-life certainly has a particular set of challenges when we find ourselves if not exactly lost in a dark wood, then certainly less confident, more hesitant and perhaps depressed. 'Everything that was nailed down has come loose,' says David Maitland.[56] Old certainties suddenly seem flimsy. 'The slings and arrows of outrageous fortune' that Hamlet bemoans provoke questions that are profoundly unsettling. We wake up to the fact that there are fewer years in which to discover solid certainties. We are not immortal.

Carl Jung characterizes this awakening as a 'second journey'. 'Wholly unprepared,' he says, 'we embark upon the second half of life ... We take this step with the false assumption that our truths and ideals will serve us as hitherto. But we cannot live the afternoon of life according to the programme of life's morning: for what in the morning was true, will at evening have become a lie.'[57] 'Lie' may be too strong a word. Circumstances and situations change, and with them one's reasons for following one course of action and not pursuing another, but this does not invalidate the choices we made in the mornings of our life. I have never regretted my decision either to enter monastic life or to leave it, though it was harder to leave than to join because of the network of relationships that had been forged over many years.

In the days after I left the monastery, words of Thomas Merton from his *Thoughts in Solitude* took on a startling immediacy:

> My Lord God, I have no idea where I am going. I do not see the road ahead of me. I cannot know where it will end. Nor do I really know myself, and the fact that I think that I am following your will does not mean that I am actually doing so. But I believe that the desire to please you does in fact please you. And I hope I have that desire in all that I am doing. I hope that I will never do anything apart from that desire. And I know that if I do this, you will lead me by the right road, though I may know nothing about it. Therefore, I will trust you always, though I may seem to be lost in the

shadow of death. I will not fear, for you are ever with me, and you will never leave me to face my perils alone.[58]

Merton encouraged me to think that God was in the chaos and confusion of my leaving, though most of the time – at least in those early months – I did not believe this. Happiness, like God, seemed impossibly far off, the far side of a succession of obstacles I had yet to overcome. I had little hope of circumstances ever changing sufficiently to allow the possibility of recovering a degree of equilibrium. It felt as if my internal filing cabinet had burst open. Files representing different parts of my life were scattered all over the floor and, try as I might, I could not get them back into any meaningful order. They no longer fitted in the filing cabinet. I felt exposed, vulnerable to people's scrutiny. Eventually I gave up trying to 'sort things'. Instead of trying to 'understand' what was happening, I learned to 'stand under' the experience and let it sort me. The pressure to 'keep up appearances', however, was huge, but Dylan Thomas's 'force that through the green fuse drives the flower' spoke to me of new possibilities and creativity, of new patterns of life emerging. Eventually, green shoots did indeed start to poke through the mud.

The road less travelled

The American poet Robert Frost spent the years 1912–15 in England, during which time he became a close friend and confidant of the poet and essayist Edward Thomas, best known for his evocative depictions of English rural life. The two men enjoyed walking in the countryside, and it is said that on one such occasion they came to an unexpected fork in the road. Unsure about which way to go, they argued about which was the best route, with Thomas subsequently insisting that they should have chosen the other road. Frost returned to New Hampshire in 1915, acquiring a hut in remote woodland close to his home and to which he could retreat and write. In a clearing in the trees below his hut, the forest trail divides, one footpath climbing the hillside, the other descending to the valley below. We do not know whether it was this scene or the memory of his walk with his old friend that inspired Frost to write his poem 'The Road Not Taken', but we do know that he sent Edward Thomas an advance copy. Thomas took the poem seriously and personally, and it may have played a part in his decision to enlist and fight in World War One. Tragically, he was killed at the Battle of Arras in 1917.

> Two roads diverged in a yellow wood,
> And sorry I could not travel both
> And be one traveler, long I stood
> And looked down one as far as I could
> To where it bent in the undergrowth;
>
> Then took the other, as just as fair,
> And having perhaps the better claim,
> Because it was grassy and wanted wear;
> Though as for that the passing there
> Had worn them really about the same,
>
> And both that morning equally lay
> In leaves no step had trodden black.
> Oh, I kept the first for another day!
> Yet knowing how way leads on to way,
> I doubted if I should ever come back.

> I shall be telling this with a sigh
> Somewhere ages and ages hence:
> Two roads diverged in a wood, and I –
> I took the one less traveled by,
> And that has made all the difference.[59]

When we are confronted by a fork in the road, we cannot go down both paths: we have to choose. As I observed earlier, there is an irrevocability about the choices we make. In the words of the ancient Greek philosopher Heraclitus, 'You can never step into the same river twice.'[60] We walk in such light as we have. We cannot afford to wait until everything becomes crystal clear before making a decision because it never will. No decision is risk-free. We have to jump. In times of bewilderment and uncertainty, all we can do is respond as best we can to the glimmers of light we see. But as we venture into the unknown, we do gain a degree of clarity and a sense of direction. The initial recognition of what to do invites us to take a step forward, and that tentative move leads to further recognition and another step, and so our journey continues.

With the passing of years, we learn to live with our choices, sometimes contentedly so like Robert Frost, at other times with a degree of regret. In our later years, our options become fewer and our freedom to choose more limited. The closing down of possibility is part of the challenge of growing older. Coming to terms with the past and how we view the limitations of the present determines whether we enjoy a sense of fulfilment or end up sour and resentful. Although the circumstances of our life may be less open to change, what is always open to change is how we choose to view our situation, including the decisions we made in the mornings of our life and the roads we did not take. Whenever I find myself in pensive mood, reviewing my life and sifting my memories, I pray that God will liberate me from being trapped in cycles of endless self-recrimination. Admitting that part of one's life is over is hard. The invitation from God is always upwards and into grace: it is an invitation to let go and to trust.

The themes of journey, failure, trust and recovery weave their way through the story of Jonah as he rebels against the call of God to travel to Nineveh and denounce their evil ways. Unsurprisingly, he is frightened and feels overwhelmed by self-doubt and the scale of the task. It drives him to flee not only God but his home, his family and perhaps himself into the bargain. But Jonah the loser is also Jonah the finder: he discovers not only an unexpected resilience but also the depth and breadth of God's love. For Jonah, shipwrecked and at sea, the sting of death was not the loss of life but the loss of meaning.

Choosing life

Writing in the fourth century about his own journey through life, Hilary, Bishop of Poitiers, says, 'We have been given life in order to achieve something worthwhile. At first, I was attracted by the pursuit of wealth and leisure. But, as most people discover, human nature wants something better to do than gourmandise and kill time. We have been given life in order to achieve something worthwhile, to make good use of our talents.'[61] Hilary echoes the wisdom of St Paul: 'They are to do good, to be rich in good works, generous, and ready to share, thus storing up for themselves the treasure of a good foundation for the future, so that they may take hold of the life that really is life.'[62] His language, and in particular his phrase 'a life worth living', *vita vitalis*, first appear 300 years earlier in Cicero.[63] The Latin phrase is a version of an even older Greek phrase. What makes life worthwhile? What gives it meaning? As we have noted, they are the same questions that centuries later John Locke and Thomas Jefferson wrestled with in their generation.

Philosophers, ancient and modern, offer contrasting answers to these big existential questions, but most agree that human beings are made for relationship. We need to belong. Friendship, marriage and family life are fundamental to human happiness and are the building blocks of a stable society. It is why, in Hilary's view, identifying what makes life worth living and what makes us happy must never be reduced to a quest for personal enlightenment: it is an enterprise for the whole of society. And in this enterprise, faith and religion have a part to play because they shape a distinctive understanding of human flourishing.

There is always a danger of reading the Bible through twenty-first-century spectacles, but there is no doubt that those living in the Hebrew world had a rich understanding of humanity. Most importantly, 'person' did not equate to an 'individual' as we instinctively might think. The Hebrew word for 'man', *'adam*, is used in two ways. It means both a person *and* humankind; there is a collective dimension to the word. I only become a person through relatedness. In contemporary western society, the ethos of individualism and the exaltation of free choice makes this perspective seem old-fashioned. As heirs of the Enlightenment, our outlook is unconsciously shaped by Descartes: 'I think, therefore I am.'

In contrast to this individualistic mindset, the African philosophy of *ubuntu*, which emphasizes interconnectedness within a community and promotes collective responsibility, has shaped an outlook that is closer to the biblical one. Unlike Descartes, it says, 'I am because we are.' The life-values of traditional African culture infuse a community-based understanding of happiness, evident in the continent's most famous proverb, 'It takes a village to raise a child.' Human identity is shaped by our relationships. In the West we seem to have lost this grand vision of inter-relatedness, and it lies at the root of much discontent. The gospel of individualism says 'I do not need my neighbour to be myself.' It sees the other either as a means to an end or as an obstacle to personal fulfilment. Contrast Antony of the Desert, one of the early Christian monastics who peopled the deserts of Egypt, Palestine and Syria in the fourth and fifth centuries, who famously said, 'Our life and our death are with our neighbour.'

Another African proverb reminds me that my conflicts and pleasures affect others and the world I live in: 'When elephants fight, the grass gets hurt. When two elephants make love, it's not good for the lawn.' Don't be deceived; your relationships and choices have consequences for other people's wellbeing: you cannot afford to be remote from the injustices and inequalities of the world. Perceived unfairness is certainly a cause of discontent. From an African perspective, western society has become lost in dark woods, the right road lost, because we exalt the individual at the expense of the communal and glamorize the young at the expense of the old. We divorce personal autonomy and human rights from social responsibility and community.

'I have set before you today life and prosperity, death and adversity ... Choose life so that you and your descendants may live, loving the LORD your God, obeying him, and holding fast to him.'[64] As the Israelites prepared to enter the Promised Land, Moses set before them a series of choices. In the Bible, 'choosing life' is not one consumer choice among others. It is about living by wholesome values which enable us to live creatively. It is about being in a right relationship with our neighbour and our Creator and knowing that we ourselves are worthwhile. We are not atoms floating in a sea of chaos or chance. The universe is about relationship, not randomness. We are made to know God and to enjoy God for ever.

The faultline

Unfortunately, there is an anomaly in human behaviour that militates against this. As Augustine noted centuries ago: 'Man wishes to be happy even when he so lives as to make happiness impossible.'[65] Augustine is telling me something I don't want to hear. Scientists rightly draw my attention to the part that genes and early upbringing play in shaping attitudes and aspirations. They point to the way our upbringing, particularly in our early years, can predispose some more than others to happiness. Nurture is as influential as nature. But Augustine is also right: I can wreck my chances of happiness by the way I live. There is, he says, a faultline in humanity, a self-destructive tendency that runs through each of us. We want to be happy and fulfilled, but we destroy our chances by the choices we make.

Modern brain-imaging studies confirm that certain behaviours show up in the size and functionality of different areas in the brain. But these studies also show that not only does our brain shape our behaviour, but our behaviour shapes our brain. There is a growing understanding of the way genes can be switched on and off by our environment and the way we respond to it. Human behaviour is complex, and the environment, experience and human choice are as much a part of the picture as biological susceptibility. And it is precisely in this arena that our spirituality is forged, where needs and wants, desire and choice fight it out.

It is easy to caricature Augustine as a grumpy killjoy, but key words in his lexicon are delight, desire and love. He recognizes in these strong, confusing and (at times) frightening energies hallmarks of our common humanity. He grapples with questions that perplex us all: what do I desire and long for? What do I delight in? What do I love? One of Augustine's favourite verses in the psalms is 'LORD, all my desires are known to you.'[66] We all have needs and longings and God knows them all. The problem lies not with God but with us: we do not know what we want. This is why, in the recurring conflict of desire and choice, we need God's help to make good decisions and identify the right road ahead – even if the road we end up choosing is one that is less travelled.

There is an inescapable loneliness in making life-choices and, in our vulnerability, Isaiah offers these words of reassurance:

Though the LORD may give you the bread of adversity and the water of affliction, yet your Teacher will not hide himself any more, but your eyes shall see your Teacher. And when you turn to the right or when you turn to the left, your ears shall hear a word behind you, saying, 'This is the way; walk in it.'[67]

For Dante, there are things to be discovered in times of suffering and vulnerability. 'It is hard to speak about what it was like in those dense thickets,' he says in an exhausted voice, 'the woods so tangled and rough, that the very thought of it renews my panic. But to rehearse the good it also brought me, I will speak of the other things I discovered.'[68] Dante wants us to understand what Jonah also discovered: that, by God's grace, good things can come from dreadful times. When we lose our way in dark woods, the right road lost, we certainly get to know ourselves better. We are forced to search for a life worth living. Sometimes, in the very moments that seem to deny the possibility of hope, we discover new things about life, about others, about ourselves and about God. We have no option but to trust and to trust and to trust.

And it can make 'all the difference'.

Reflections

- Can you think of a time in your life when you were confronted by a fork in the road? What did it feel like? What helped you choose the path you did?

- Many of us live with a sense of having made a wrong or poor decision in the past. How do we understand this in the light of St Paul's conviction that 'all things work together for good for those who love God' (Rom. 8.28)?

- What has helped you pray in a time of bewilderment?

O Holy Spirit, whose presence is liberty, grant us that freedom which will not fear to tread unknown ways, nor be held back by misgivings of ourselves or the fear of others. Ever beckon us forward to the place of thy will which is also the place of thy power, O ever-leading, ever-loving Lord.

George Appleton (1902–93)

As the rain hides the stars,
as the autumn mist hides the hills,
as the clouds veil the blue sky,
so the dark happenings of my lot hide the shining of
 thy face from me.
Yet, if I may hold thy hand in the darkness, it is enough
since I know that, though I may stumble in my going,
 thou dost not fall.

> Gaelic Prayer

God grant me grace to accept with serenity
the things that cannot be changed,
the courage to change the things that I can,
and the wisdom to know the difference.

> Reinhold Niebuhr (1892–1971)

O the mind, mind has mountains; cliffs of fall
Frightful, sheer, no-man-fathomed. Hold them cheap
May who ne'er hung there.

> Gerard Manley Hopkins (1844–89)
> 'No Worst, There Is None'

4
Out of the depths

Jonah is thrown overboard by the crew and there is a great calm, but miraculously he does not drown. Instead, we are told, God 'provides' a large fish to swallow him, and he is taken down into the depths. It is the stuff of nightmares. The Hebrews believed that the earth was founded on a vast subterranean ocean and that the roots of the mountains, the pillars of the earth, went down into water – into the floods, as they were called. The psalms are peppered with references to the floods. To give just three examples: 'The floods have lifted up, O LORD, the floods have lifted up their voice' (Ps. 93.3). 'The LORD sits enthroned above the flood' (Ps. 29.10). 'I have come into deep waters and the flood sweeps over me' (Ps. 69.2). They are all references to the primeval soup out of which God was believed to have brought forth light, order and peace. In other words, in the image of the storm and of Jonah being thrown into the raging waters, and then being taken down into the belly of a great sea monster, we are being presented with a metaphor for spiritual chaos and of death itself.

It is why Jesus, in his acrimonious exchange with the scribes, chooses Jonah's descent into the belly of the whale as 'the sign', the supreme image of his own forthcoming dereliction and death. More than that, because Jonah does not drown, it also embodies an oblique reference to the possibility of resurrection: 'As Jonah was three days and three nights in the belly of the sea monster, so shall the Son of Man be in the heart of the earth' (Matt. 12.40). There is no doubt that Jesus's contemporaries recognized the force of the allusion he was making, even if (as is likely) they did not grasp the implications of what he was trying to communicate. But what of Jonah's cry for help and the psalm he prays from the belly of the fish?

> The LORD provided a large fish to swallow up Jonah; and Jonah was in the belly of the fish for three days and three nights. Then Jonah prayed to the LORD his God from the belly of the fish, saying,
>
>> 'I called to the LORD out of my distress,
>> and he answered me;
>> out of the belly of Sheol I cried,
>> and you heard my voice.
>> You cast me into the deep,
>> into the heart of the seas,
>> and the flood surrounded me;
>> all your waves and your billows
>> passed over me.
>> Then I said, "I am driven away
>> from your sight;
>> how shall I look again
>> upon your holy temple?"
>> The waters closed in over me;
>> the deep surrounded me;
>> weeds were wrapped around my head

> at the roots of the mountains.
> I went down to the land
> whose bars closed upon me for ever;
> yet you brought up my life from the Pit,
> O LORD my God.
> As my life was ebbing away,
> I remembered the LORD;
> and my prayer came to you,
> into your holy temple.
> Those who worship vain idols
> forsake their true loyalty.
> But I with the voice of thanksgiving
> will sacrifice to you;
> what I have vowed I will pay.
> Deliverance belongs to the LORD!'

> Then the LORD spoke to the fish, and it spewed Jonah out upon the dry land.[69]

From the heart of darkness Jonah prays to God. His psalm has strong parallels with two psalms in the Psalter: Psalm 130, the so-called *de profundis* ('Out of the depths have I called to you, O LORD'), and Psalm 69 ('Save me, O God, because the waters have come up to my throat'). In medieval manuscripts, monastic scribes creating illuminated Psalters made a ready link between the plight of Jonah and Psalm 69, often depicting Jonah curled up inside the initial 'S' of *Salvum*, the opening word of the psalm in Latin. All three psalms are full of pain and anguish, pleas to God for help and mercy, but there are differences as well as similarities between Jonah's prayer and the other two psalms. In

Jonah's psalm we have a poem about what happens when we feel overwhelmed by our internal chaos, when we feel out of our depth.

Jonah's prayer to God is a cry of desolation: 'The floods closed in over me; the deep surrounded me. Weeds were wrapped around my head at the roots of the mountains. I went down to the land whose bars closed upon me forever.' The Hebrew word *suph* is usually translated, as here in the NRSV, as 'weeds' or even 'seaweed' but is more accurately translated as 'reeds'. The word is Egyptian in origin and occurs twice in the Book of Exodus: first, for the reeds growing along the banks of the Nile where the baby Moses floated safely in a basket; and, second, in Exodus 15, for the 'Sea of Reeds' through which the Israelites cross dry shod in their flight from Pharaoh and his chariots as they journey to the Promised Land. There is a wordplay going on here. Jonah feels he is drowning in chaos, engulfed by the primeval waters that signal destruction and death but, like the escaping Israelites before him, Yahweh is in the process of saving him. God is leading Jonah on to dry ground and safety.

The early Christians recognized the force of the symbolism and, in their iconography and liturgy, made links of their own. They saw in Jonah's descent into the water a type of baptism: submerged beneath the waves, Jonah moves from death to life. He is re-born. In a similar way, the Christian is immersed in the waters of baptism and sacramentally united with Christ in his dying and rising. It is why the early Christians painted Jonah immersed in water on the walls of the catacombs of the dead in Rome, proclaiming their hope of a resurrection to eternal life. It is also why, since early days, many Christian lectionaries have appointed this second chapter of the Book of Jonah, with its psalm of dereliction, to be read on Holy Saturday, the day of silent emptiness suspended between Good Friday and Easter Day, between crucifixion and resurrection.

In the paradox of grace, Jonah's traumatic experience of being thrown overboard and nearly drowning is his salvation. It is his personal exodus to freedom and new life. His psalm is written in its own theological counterpoint: it is both a prayer of protest *and* a song of thanksgiving to the God who saves. His protest echoes the comment of Teresa of Avila, the Spanish Carmelite and mystic, who, travelling on the back of an ox cart across the Sierra Nevada during her visitation of her Order's convents, is alleged to have said, 'Well, God, if this is how you treat your friends, it is small wonder that you have so few of them.'

Praying the psalms with Jonah

> Nourished by the Scriptures, we should learn to penetrate so deeply into the meaning of the psalms that we sing them not as though they had been composed by the prophet, but as if we ourselves had written them, as if this psalm were our own personal prayer to God, uttered amid the deepest compunction of our heart. We should think of the psalms as having been specially composed for us, and recognize that what they are expressing is real, not simply historically so in the life and person of the prophet, but now, today, as they are fulfilled in our own lives.[70]

So writes John Cassian, monk and theologian, at the end of the fourth century. The more I meditate on the psalms, the more I too applaud their range of emotion. We encounter praise, anger, fear, frustration, passion, hatred, sadness, hope, despair, desolation, joy. The psalms provide us with a rich vocabulary with which to pray, praise and lament. They give us permission to feel before God. They allow us to protest at the injustices of life, to be angry in the face of cruelty, to lament the death of a friend, to be ourselves before God in our confusion. They rail against the silence of God, his apparent indifference to the suffering in the world. Many of the psalms relate to the perennial but unanswerable question: why do bad things happen to good people?

When I was a vicar in north London in an area with a large Jewish population, I got to know the local rabbis well. I remember discussing prayer with one of them and the rabbi saying: 'The trouble with you Christians is that you are far too polite to God'. There is a robustness about the way Jews pray that is both challenging and energizing. They are less deferential to the Almighty than Christians. Jews are neither ashamed nor afraid to express raw emotion before God whereas Christians tend to edit their feelings, particularly anger. Sometimes we are so afraid of our anger that we deny its existence and suppress it behind false smiles, with the result that it smoulders just below the surface, occasionally flaring out in the occasional cutting remark.

Some editions of the psalms prepared for liturgical use place verses expressing anger and violence in square brackets with the recommendation that they are omitted. There are certainly challenges about how we appropriate such psalms in public worship, but if we edit out the angry bits, where do we stop? Why not cut out the conceited and smug bits too? We would do better to take to heart the words of Albany spoken at the close of Shakespeare's *King Lear*: 'Speak what we feel, not what we ought to say.'[71] When reciting a psalm, we may not be going through what Jonah or the Psalmist is describing but, as John Cassian says, they are expressing what is real. In the case of psalms of desolation, we pray in solidarity with all who feel abused, victimized, marginalized or abandoned.

In Alan Bennett's play *The History Boys*, the boys moan at Hector, their eccentric history teacher, about having to learn poetry by heart. 'Sir,' complains one pupil, 'I don't always understand poetry.' To which Hector replies, 'I *never* understand it. But learn it now, know it now, and you'll understand it whenever.' 'But,' insists the boy, 'I don't see how we can understand it. Most of the stuff poetry's about hasn't happened to us yet.' 'But it will,' replies Hector. 'It will. And then you will have the antidote ready. Grief. Happiness. Even when you're dying.'[72] What Hector says of poetry and the merit of learning it by heart could equally be said of the psalms. With time and frequent repetition, they form an inner library, a compendium of lived experience, providing us with a spiritual vocabulary with which to pray in times of sadness and joy or when words fail us.

The psalms allow us to name what may be going on around us or inside us: in the world, in our local community, in our own family, in our own hearts. We should not edit what we feel or worry that it might not be acceptable to the Almighty. God can cope. The sanitized path is grey and it leads to spiritual death. Faith is not resignation in the face of life's tragedies. Faith is the fruit of the struggle to act and pray honestly. We pray as we are, not as we would like to be. It takes time and effort to be elegant in prayer, but only honesty and humility to be real. I'm sure God prefers our prayer to be real rather than elegant.

God the disruptor

In times of crisis, we instinctively cast God in the role of comforter, in part because the fourth Gospel describes the Holy Spirit as *parakletos* – variously translated from the Greek as 'advocate', 'counsellor' or 'comforter'. But Jonah encounters God as a source not of reassurance and peace, but of *discomfort*. God is the great disturber, the disruptor of his plans, who shakes him (and us) out of his lethargy and complacency. God thwarts Jonah's escape plans to Tarshish first by causing the storm and then by 'providing' a giant fish to swallow him. Trapped in the belly of the fish, Jonah has ample opportunity to contemplate his fate. He has messed up and feels useless, but God doesn't allow him to wallow in self-pity. God has plans for him. Jonah feels he is drowning, but he is not. Yahweh is graciously saving him, which is why the psalm ends with a resounding cry of redemption: 'Deliverance belongs to the LORD.'[73]

Prayer can be a bewildering experience. We find ourselves moving from knowing about God to knowing God. We move from comparative clarity into opaqueness. We exchange a feeling of confidence, that we know where we are and what we are doing, for uncertainty. Was that prayer? we ask ourselves. We find ourselves in a relationship in which it is easy to lose our bearings and feel out of our depth, where trust is the only way forward.

I easily get distracted when I pray. My mind wanders and, before I know it, I am thinking about what to cook for dinner or the problem with my car's exhaust. The word 'distraction' derives from the Latin *distrahere*, meaning to drag away. But from what am I being dragged away? One of the reasons my prayer sometimes goes stale is not the absence of God but the absence of me. I am not engaged; I am not present.

Psychologists often picture our inner world as a river. On this analogy, the adventure of prayer is akin to crossing it on a rickety rope bridge. From time to time, we get distracted by the flotsam and jetsam passing below in the swirling water: memories, questions, worries, thoughts about the day ahead vie for our attention. The challenge is to keep looking ahead and allow the debris to drift on downstream without giving it undue attention. Except what if the flotsam and jetsam is the real stuff of prayer? What if, when I pray, God is trying to disrupt my escape plans and confront me with an unresolved matter in my life that needs sorting but which I am wilfully ignoring? What then? Far from being a distraction, might not this be the true agenda of prayer?

The French Jesuit Jean-Pierre de Caussade (1675–1751), in his letters of spiritual direction to the Visitation nuns of Nancy, many of which were later collated and circulated under the title *Abandonment to Divine Providence*, encourages us to pray for the gift of discernment in the face of distraction. He urges us to bring the untidiness of our lives into the heart of our prayer, including that which appears to contradict God's purposes of love. He exhorts us to be 'actively passive' to the action of God. Faith, he says, is like a scalpel which dissects painful experiences: 'It cuts through these appearances, grasping the hand of God who keeps us alive.'[74] Such surgery of the soul is energized by the conviction that God is to be discovered in the mess and pain, holding out his own wounded hands. It was de Caussade who coined the phrase 'the sacrament of the present moment' to describe how the will of God can be embraced in every moment of every day and how this can transform our whole outlook on life.

Praying from a place of vulnerability

In his book *A Season for the Spirit*,[75] Martin Smith tells the story of the rediscovery of an ancient therapeutic spring in Worcestershire. Tradition located the spring in the vicinity of White Ladies Aston, a village that took its name from a medieval convent of white-habited Cistercian nuns in the area. In the Middle Ages people with eye diseases used to go on pilgrimage to its holy well seeking healing. With the Dissolution of the Monasteries in the sixteenth century, all trace of the spring was lost. There had been an attempt to locate it in the Edwardian period, but without success. Martin Smith describes his own unsuccessful attempts to find the spring until it occurred to him that the cows, standing in the muddy corner of one of the fields, might be guarding the secret. He describes prodding and digging in the dung and how eventually his trowel grated against stone. Later that day he gently uncovered an intricately carved stone platform from which protruded a small lead pipe. He cleaned out the mud from the pipe and out gushed pure water. It was the medieval spring, the place of pilgrimage and healing.

His discovery echoes words of Jesus in St John's Gospel: 'The water that I will give will become in them a spring of water, gushing up to eternal life.'[76] And again later in the Gospel: 'On the last day of the festival, the great day, while Jesus was standing there, he cried out, "Let anyone who is thirsty come to me, and let the one who believes in me drink. As the scripture has said, 'Out of the believer's heart shall flow rivers of living water.'" Now he said this about the Spirit, which believers in him were to receive; for as yet there was no Spirit, because Jesus was not yet glorified.'[77]

The phrase *ek tes koilias* is usually translated (as above) 'out of the [believer's] heart', but the Greek is more accurately translated as guts. *Kardia*, the Greek word for heart, is not used here by the fourth Evangelist. The word is *koilias*, meaning the viscera or the womb. Interestingly, of all the English translations only the King James Bible (AV) renders the verse accurately: 'Out of your belly shall flow rivers of living water.' The word 'belly' captures the grit of Jesus's words. In the Septuagint, the Greek version of the Old Testament, the same word is used for the belly of the whale from which Jonah prays to God. Place these two texts side by side and an interesting convergence of ideas emerges. It suggests that the home of the Holy Spirit is not the intellect, the realm of concepts and ideas, but the guts – the deep inner core where our passions have their origin. It is the place of conflict, confusion, protest, vulnerability and desire. This is the place from which, like Jonah, we pray our deepest prayers.

The Edwardian expedition failed to locate the medieval spring, perhaps because it never occurred to them that a muddy corner of a field, encrusted with dung, could be disguising such a holy place. We too often pass over the place of the Spirit's indwelling in our lives: to quote Smith, 'that unpromising and murky place of our guts'. We prefer to look for the Spirit in the cleaner, sanitized world of thought and piety, but the Spirit is to be found in the core of our humanity, summoning us to life as once God summoned Jonah: 'Get up. Arise. We have a journey to go on.'

And the fish spewed Jonah out upon the dry land.

Reflections

For God alone my soul waits in silence;
  from him comes my salvation.
He alone is my rock and my salvation, my fortress;
  I shall never be shaken. (Psalm 62.1)

- Spend some time browsing through the book of Psalms, waiting on God in silence. Is there a psalm that speaks to you today?

- As you reflect on God's challenge to be real, why not compose your own psalm? It could be a lament, a prayer of protest such as Jonah prayed from the belly of the whale, or a psalm of praise and thanksgiving. Unlike English poetry, the psalmists were not concerned about rhyme. Instead, they often said the same thing twice but in different ways. The contrasting images they chose were mutually illuminating. Adopting the Hebrew convention, what words and images describe the landscape of your heart and your own journey of faith?

Nobody heard him, the dead man,
But still he lay moaning:
I was much further out than you thought
And not waving but drowning.

Poor chap, he always loved larking
And now he's dead
It must have been too cold for him his heart gave way,
They said.

Oh, no no no, it was too cold always
(Still the dead one lay moaning)
I was much too far out all my life
And not waving but drowning.

Stevie Smith (1902–71)
'Not Waving but Drowning'[78]

5
Not waving but drowning

In his novel *The Hours*, Michael Cunningham describes how Clarissa Vaughan, a 52-year-old publisher living a comfortable existence with her long-term partner, Sally, steps out of her smart Greenwich Village apartment in New York to buy flowers for a party she is hosting. An accomplished businesswoman, Clarissa appears happy and successful but feels shallow and superficial. She is haunted by the memory of the early days of her friendship with Richard, when she perceived herself to have been so much more alive than she is now. She remembers their first embrace and fantasizes about what might have been:

> It had seemed like the beginning of happiness, and Clarissa is still sometimes shocked, more than thirty years later, to realise that it *was* happiness; that the entire experience lay in a kiss and a walk, the anticipation of dinner and a book ... There is still that singular perfection, and it's perfect in part because it seemed, at the time, so clearly to promise more. Now she knows. That was the moment, right then. There has been no other.[79]

Often the first glimmer that 'things aren't right' occurs when the ordinary things of life cease to give us pleasure. Life loses its lustre. We feel bewildered and restless. An underlying unhappiness increasingly fills our waking hours. Discontent can register in various shades of grey, descending into the blackness of depression. It may be accompanied by a sense of nostalgia. Like Clarissa Vaughan, we look back and perceive ourselves to have been happy – only somehow we missed it. It slipped through our fingers like sand on the beach, and we curse our stupidity.

It is possible to have been miserable for years but never admit it. For all sorts of reasons, we deceive ourselves and sometimes enlist our friends in the deception. We find ways of numbing the pain and avoiding self-scrutiny, perhaps because we are frightened of disturbing the status quo. In some cases, the strategies we adopt can be so successful that we end up no longer knowing what we feel about anything. Consciously or unconsciously, we have pressed the deep-freeze button. Even negative and self-destructive situations begin to seem comforting simply because they are predictable and familiar. If they draw power from any latent feelings of poor self-esteem, then our inertia is complete. We batten down the hatches. We fear to open up lest we be overwhelmed by a deluge of unnamed doubts and fears.

Most of the time we manage to keep our heads above water, even occasionally waving at friends in a jolly sort of way. But inside we feel we are sinking and are frightened our friends will realize too late that, like Stevie Smith, we haven't been waving at all but drowning. Her poem speaks not only of her own loneliness, but of the loneliness she observes in others. It echoes the anguish of Clarissa Vaughan and of a nun I once knew who told me that she was 'crying on the inside of my face, only no one noticed'. All three women lived with a sense of isolation, their sadness compounded by the daily burden that those closest to them seemed remote and unaware of their desolation. Self-deception is something for which each of us must take responsibility, but what is truly dispiriting is when the people we love trivialize our misery or simply don't notice.

Attending a seminar on alcoholism, drug abuse and compulsive gambling, I was told that various factors drive addiction, ranging from high levels of anxiety among young professionals to the deep discontent felt by those who are forced to endure a joyless existence in terrible housing with little to do and no prospect of change. Apparently the two most potent factors are poor self-esteem and unhappiness at home. Boredom and feelings of discontent are magnified by the unrealistic expectations that advertising and social media foster. People feel left out or left behind. Rationally, we know that we can't be happy all the time, but emotionally we assume that something has gone wrong. It is no coincidence that pubs and clubs regularly advertise 'happy hours'. It may be a marketing ploy, but it draws power from the unquestioned assumption that happiness is there for the taking.

When we are unhappy and no longer feel at home in ourselves, it is tempting to reach for a trusted anaesthetic. Unfortunately, as our tolerance of analgesia grows, we can find ourselves increasing the dose lest the pain break through. We are putting our feet on the slippery slope that leads to breakdown, burn-out or addiction. In isolation, a decision not to reach for our trusty anaesthetic or to collude with self-destructive patterns of behaviour may seem insignificant, but it can be a step on the road that will lead us out of the thicket of Dante's 'dark woods'.

Drug-taking is rarely seen as a moral issue for young people. It is 'recreational', part of the leisure industry that is busy re-creating us as a nation of happy people. Here are things that will blot out the downside of life. They promise self-confidence and wellbeing, albeit a wellbeing that is chemically induced and temporary. There are plenty of anaesthetics on the market beside drugs. Overwork, pornography, shopping, compulsive exercising and comfort-eating may be less obvious drugs, but they can be equally addictive and damaging. Even religion and caring for others can become displacement activities. There is a false style of living in which we appear to be living for others, but are in fact assuaging our own deep despair. If we are unsure of being accepted and loved by others, we can compensate by looking after an endless succession of people. That way, we avoid the need to face ourselves and our own need of love.

Living without anaesthetics

Some people talk and write about happiness as if what we should strive for is a sort of impregnability or invulnerability. They describe a version of life I do not recognize. Grief, disappointment, loneliness and suffering are not medical disorders: they are part of life. In our culture sadness is fast becoming a taboo subject. It is as if there is a prohibition gathering around the very use of the word. We even use the term pejoratively: 'He's a sad case' or 'That's a sad thing to say'. We hesitate to express sadness, as if admitting to it constitutes a negative statement about ourselves. We feel ashamed, embarrassed, inadequate and, in some indefinable way, a failure. Feeling sad does not demean us and we should never fear to admit it. Naming our sadness is part of the process of learning to cope with 'unhappiness' in ways that are not self-destructive. For some, it will include pressing the 'defrost button' to allow themselves to feel again, which can be more difficult than one might think – particularly if they have become used to suppressing uncomfortable feelings. It will mean abandoning tricks of self-deception and facing bits of ourselves we find distasteful. For most of us, this will not entail coming to terms with anything extraordinary, but it will entail a high degree of personal scrutiny.

An unusual litmus test of our progress will be how we handle silence and solitude. They are gifts, but they can be intimidating because they expose inner emptiness. In the silence of the monastery, I became acutely conscious of various chattering voices inside me competing for attention. At times it felt as if discordant music was being played backwards inside my head. We long for peace and quiet, for 'space'. But if we are not at peace with ourselves, what we experience is not the gift of silence but its terror and, like Jonah, we run away. Bizarrely, we can find ourselves craving noise and company rather than face the void within. We take refuge in other people or in busyness or both. Before long, we are back in those dark woods.

There may be a link between current high levels of stress and anxiety, and the way our culture shuns silence. In silence there is not the same opportunity for egoism, by which much frightening and aching emptiness is concealed. These days we blot out silence with 'muzak' in restaurants, pubs, doctors' surgeries, railway stations and post office queues. Even classical music is regularly packaged in response to a need to escape life, 'to chill'. But what is the point of such remedial action if we do not recognize how we are fuelling our stress by the way we live?

What is driving us?

It is a commonplace to speak of a 'driven person', by which we mean someone who has become a victim of their compulsions. Instinctively, we steer clear of such people, recognizing that they are not at peace with themselves. We become protective of our own wellbeing, anxious not to get sucked into their destructive world. It may be that they are driven by a need to succeed, to be a hero – or, worse, a martyr. We recognize 'driven-ness' in others, but can we recognize it in ourselves? Perhaps a few pen-portraits might help?

Perfectionism is one manifestation and it is stoked by anxiety. We are consumed by the need to 'get it right' all the time and seem unable to recognize when something, although not perfect, is good enough. We may be afraid of censure, or it may be poor self-esteem generating an insatiable need to gain approval. It is natural to want to be loved and accepted, but sometimes we can end up being controlled by our need to be needed. This skews our relationships and inhibits our capacity to relate to others in an adult way.

There are control-freaks. As we enter adulthood, we learn to observe boundaries and to exercise appropriate control in relation to ourselves and to others, but there are those whose need to do so is pathological and who are coercive. There are workaholics, unable to leave the office because they feel insecure in their work or threatened by colleagues. Less obvious are those who take refuge in work to avoid going home and facing loneliness or domestic tension. Work begins as an excuse, becomes an escape and ends up as a prison. They find themselves trapped in a syndrome of their own creation. Then there are exhibitionists, who crave an audience, a platform on which to perform, and who suffer withdrawal symptoms until they secure their next shot of adulation but mistrust the adulation when it comes.

These amateur pen-portraits indicate some of the pitfalls to discovering 'the life that really is life' and why we can end up bewildered, much further out in life than we thought and 'not waving but drowning'. If you are like me, you will recognize bits of yourself in some of these pen-portraits. Self-recognition can be depressing, but if we can look at ourselves with a rueful but kindly eye, it is a sign of psychological health. It is a truism of counselling that what we reject in others often proceeds from what we reject in ourselves. Our search for meaning, purpose and happiness, therefore, must include not just self-awareness but self-acceptance. We need to recognize and identify what we project on to others and grow in self-understanding. If we can do this, by God's grace we will discover a new tolerance and compassion for others and be more at peace with ourselves.

Revisiting childhood memories

Self-destructive patterns often have their roots in our early years, and some of us may need to revisit childhood memories to find a way out of our 'dark woods'. Parents want their children to be happy. If the children are happy, they're happy; if the kids are fractious and miserable, the whole household goes out of kilter. But another dynamic may also be operating: children like to please their parents. When children sense that their parents are unhappy or angry, it has a profound effect on them. Joyless parents bring up joyless children, who then repeat the process.

Children easily blame themselves for what goes wrong at home. In times of conflict or sadness in a family, parents need to be both real and responsible in handling their emotions with their children. No one can get it right all the time, and when we get it wrong we need to forgive ourselves. Certain scenarios, however, are always best avoided: such as children parenting their own parents. That unhappy experience forms a reservoir of resentment. Similarly, a parent's desire for their child to succeed and 'be happy' can be communicated so strongly that it is received as a burden. What was intended as support is experienced as pressure, and the child/teenager becomes frightened of failing and takes this fear into their adult life.

The Christian tradition has a theological term for these cycles of human dysfunctionality: original sin. The doctrine is not nearly as gloomy as its critics suggest. It recognizes that there is an inherited predisposition to self-centredness in us all, as a result of which we hurt and damage one another. But the correlative is that it's not all my fault. No one begins life with a clean slate: we inherit baggage. We are responsible for some things in life but not everything, and in this bitter-sweet realization, with God's help, we can find liberation. In his poem 'Auguries of Innocence', William Blake, the eighteenth-century poet, artist and thinker, was unflinchingly candid about the human lot:

> Man was made for Joy and Woe,
> And when this we rightly know
> Thro' the World we safely go.[80]

Enabling children and young people to grow in maturity includes helping them cope with the shock that bad things happen to good people and that not everyone can win the race. Joy and woe are indeed part of the human condition, as are grief, guilt and despair. Handling shame and embarrassment are prerequisites of personal growth. Only then through the world do 'we safely go'. Endowing children with the resources to grasp these painful realities will be a wonderful foundation for their future wellbeing.

What difference does faith make?

Religious people have the advantage of being able to draw upon the resources of their beliefs when negotiating these challenges. My old tutor used to describe grace as God's glue. 'Grace is like Bostik,' she used to say. 'It stops me falling apart inside.' Sadly, some do fall apart. Some find their faith disintegrating under pressure. Disappointed that God did not protect them from illness or suffering, they question their faith or even abandon it. Coping with the fact that faith does not immunize us from trauma is a challenge most Christians will face at some juncture in their discipleship. Sickness, marriage breakup, bankruptcy, depression, redundancy or bereavement can all precipitate profound spiritual upheaval. These events interrogate our motives: do we pray because God is God, or for what we can get out of him? If we're honest, the answer is probably both. I take refuge in the words of the prophet Isaiah: 'The servant of the LORD walks in dark places where there is no light, yet trusts in the name of the LORD and leans on his God.'[81] Like the patriarch Jacob at the Ford of Jabbok, we sometimes find ourselves wrestling with God.[82]

I never cease to be moved by the sculpture of Michelangelo. Most people instinctively think of his Pietà in St Peter's in Rome or his statue of David in the Accademia in Florence. Magnificent though the David is, what enthral me are four unfinished statues in the gallery that leads to it. Called variously 'The Wrestlers' or 'The Prisoners', the figures are only half-formed, their bodies still imprisoned in the marble. An arm emerges here, a leg there, a face only partially carved. When asked about his work, Michelangelo is alleged to have said that the sculpture already exists, trapped in the stone. His job was 'to release it by taking away that which is superfluous'. In life we come to God's bench rough-hewn, but by his hand we can be fashioned to a truer beauty. That which is superfluous in our lives will be chipped away so that we are no longer imprisoned but released to be ourselves. Our hearts may be calcified, our minds and bodies as good as dead, but God summons us to life, to become who we are. Like Jonah, there is no need for us to drown.

Reflections

- Have there been episodes in your life when you have felt yourself drowning, not waving? What helped you most during that time?

- Many of us revisit past hurts and damaging conversations from time to time. Do you have painful memories which are yet to be healed? How might you use them as the raw material for your prayer?

- Are there areas in your life from which you need to be released, 'the superfluous chipped away', to become the person God has created you to be?

Merciful God, who answers the poor, answer us.
Merciful God, who answers the lowly in spirit, answer us.
Merciful God, who answers the broken in heart, answer us.
Merciful God, answer us.
Merciful God, have compassion.
Merciful God, redeem.
Merciful God, save.
Merciful God, have pity on us, now, speedily, and at a
   near time.

       From the Liturgy for the Day of Atonement

There exist in this world two cities created by two kinds of love: the earthly city created by self-love reaching the point of contempt for God, and the heavenly city created by the love of God. The earthly city glories in itself, whereas the heavenly city glories only in its Lord. In the former, the lust for power controls its functionaries and determines the fate of the nations it subjugates; in the city of God those in authority and those under them serve one another in love.

Augustine (354–430)
The City of God, 22

6
Down and out in Nineveh

In the third chapter of the Book of Jonah we come to the nub of the story: Jonah's arrival in Nineveh and his call to its citizens to repent.

> The word of the LORD came to Jonah a second time, saying, 'Get up, go to Nineveh, that great city, and proclaim to it the message that I tell you.' So Jonah set out and went to Nineveh, according to the word of the LORD. Now Nineveh was an exceedingly large city, a three days' walk across. Jonah began to go into the city, going a day's walk. And he cried out, 'Forty days more, and Nineveh shall be overthrown!' And the people of Nineveh believed God; they proclaimed a fast, and everyone, great and small, put on sackcloth.

> When the news reached the king of Nineveh, he rose from his throne, removed his robe, covered himself with sackcloth, and sat in ashes. Then he had a proclamation made in Nineveh: 'By the decree of the king and his nobles: No human being or animal, no herd or flock, shall taste anything. They shall not feed, nor shall they drink water. Human beings and animals shall be covered with sackcloth, and they shall cry mightily to God. All shall turn from their evil ways and from the violence that is in their hands. Who knows? God may relent and change his mind; he may turn from his fierce anger, so that we do not perish.'
>
> When God saw what they did, how they turned from their evil ways, God changed his mind about the calamity that he had said he would bring upon them; and he did not do it.[83]

For a second time, God directs Jonah to Nineveh. Get up. Arise. Here is that word again! God is always telling us to get up and get going. No slacking. There is no reproach of Jonah's earlier disobedience and attempted flight, only a quiet reiteration of the command. In her *Revelations of Divine Love*, Julian of Norwich, the medieval mystic, speaks of the gentleness of God towards us:

> When we fall through our weakness or blindness, our Lord in his courtesy puts his hand on us, encourages us, and holds on to us. Only then does he will that we should see our wretchedness, and humbly acknowledge it. It is not God's intention for us to remain like this, nor that we should go to great lengths in our self-accusation, nor that we should feel too wretched about ourselves.[84]

Her words illustrate a difference between the ways of God and the way we often treat one another. God does not humiliate or demean or operate a shame and blame policy, whereas we, in our need to be in control, our need not only to be right but to be seen to be right, cannot resist point-scoring and putting in the knife. By word and gesture, we cement in the mind of the other person their inadequacy and our superiority.

'Get up, go to Nineveh, that great city, and proclaim to it the message that I tell you.'[85] And what a great city it was. It took Jonah three whole days to cross it – or so we are told. We are used to modern cities being huge, but for an ancient city to be that size seems incredible. Charles Halton, the biblical commentator, argues that the statement should be interpreted figuratively, rather than literally, in keeping with the style of the rest of the book.[86] Interestingly, what modern archaeological excavations confirm is that Nineveh and its surrounding area were indeed massive. According to the ancient Greek historian Diodorus Siculus, its circumference was 480 stadia. Given that Herodotus used to estimate that in a day's march an army could cover 150 stadia, it means that the city would have taken three days to circumnavigate, though not to cross as the text implies. Dr Thelma Akrawi, the leading Iraqi archaeologist, estimates that Nineveh and its surrounding area were between 20 and 25 miles across. Excavations have revealed the massive nature of Sennacherib's fortifications and city walls. The city had wide streets, some of which were paved, gardens, parks, canals, palaces, temples and houses. The combination of size and grandeur distinguished it from almost every other city in the ancient world. It must have been a truly amazing sight: magnificent and intimidating.

The call to repentance

The author paints a picture of our reluctant prophet bravely going into the heart of the biggest city in the ancient world and proclaiming a call to repentance – not once, but three times. 'Forty days more and Nineveh shall be overthrown!'[87] Jonah cuts a lonely, vulnerable figure as he takes his stand, reminiscent of those eccentric individuals who from time to time parade up and down our high streets with sandwich boards proclaiming 'The end is nigh'.

The Ninevites were known and feared for their gratuitous violence. They crushed the populations they conquered and ruled through a mixture of torture and terror. From various archaeological discoveries, including inscriptions, wall reliefs and other artefacts, we know that arbitrary executions, rape, ripping babies from the wombs of pregnant women, and smashing the heads of children against rocks were their preferred weapons of suppression. King Ashurnasipal II was renowned for hanging his enemies on posts, flaying them alive and then lining the city walls with their skins. The famous bronze Balawat Gates[88] depict Assyrian soldiers hacking apart captured soldiers and dismembering hands and feet. Impaled captives were lined up on display. Pillars of skewered human heads were erected to terrify people into submission. Contemporary sources record how the Ninevites forced parents to watch their children being burned alive and then killed the parents. Victims were buried up to their necks in sand and left to die of hunger and thirst or to be attacked by wild animals. The Ninevites were hated and feared in equal measure. It is why their city achieved a terrible notoriety. Entire populations would commit suicide rather than fall into their hands.[89]

The curse of violence

What is fascinating about the Book of Jonah is that the prophet simply announces to the Ninevites that their city is going to be overthrown, without spelling out the reasons for God's displeasure. It is the king who hears Jonah's call to repent and orders a general fast, and it is the king who articulates why they are under judgement: 'All shall turn from their evil ways and from the violence that is in their hands.'[90] Who knows? God may relent and change his mind; he may turn from his fierce anger, so that we do not perish. Had Jonah's proclamation stirred the conscience of the king? Violence is not usually a theme that is addressed in books of spirituality, which prefer to focus on themes of prayer, meditation, love and compassion. Yet the human propensity to resort to violence cannot be ignored, and it is a recurrent and disturbing theme in the Scriptures.

In the Book of Genesis, following Adam and Eve's disobedience and their expulsion from the Garden of Eden, we are confronted by Cain's violent assault and murder of his brother Abel.[91] Domestic violence is all too common, and today most homicides still occur in the family. Later in Genesis we learn of the flood that covered the earth and the reason God decreed it: 'And God said to Noah, "I have determined to make an end of all flesh, for the earth is filled with violence because of them; now I am going to destroy them along with the earth."'[92] In the Psalms and the Book of Proverbs we find laments and condemnation of those who perpetrate acts of violence,[93] and encounter one of the most troubling verses in the Bible when the Psalmist rails against Israel's enemies and declares: 'Happy shall they be who take your little ones and dash them against the rock!'[94] This expression of undiluted anger is in all probability a 'tit for tat' reference to the gratuitous violence perpetrated by the Assyrians. Both the major and minor prophets condemn all who act violently and dream of a time when peace will reign and violence be banished. In the words of Isaiah, 'Violence shall no more be heard in your land, devastation or destruction within your borders; you shall call your walls Salvation, and your gates Praise.'[95]

In the New Testament, Jesus's disciples are not immune from the temptation to resort to violence when, for example, they visit a Samaritan village which does not welcome them. 'Lord, do you want us to command fire to come down from heaven and consume them?' ask the brothers James and John.[96] And in the Garden of Gethsemane as Jesus is being arrested, Simon Peter grasps a sword and cuts off the ear of the High Priest's servant.[97] Violence is something Jesus repudiates. He castigates James and John for their suggestion and tells Peter to put his sword back in its sheath, 'for all who take the sword will perish by the sword'.[98]

We might feel smug because we have never physically assaulted anyone. But *chamas*, the Hebrew term for violence used here in Jonah, embraces all ways in which we violate others, including threatening behaviour, intimidation, bullying and shouting. Why do the Scriptures take such a strong line on violence? Because it is the very antithesis of love – the basis of the two great commandments to love God and our neighbour. Violence destroys. In the Gospels we meet Jesus, God's chosen, who bears the violence of the world in his own person as if he were cosmic blotting paper, soaking up the hatred and not passing it on. The First Letter of

Peter offers this commentary: 'Christ also suffered for you, leaving you an example, so that you should follow in his steps. He committed no sin, and no deceit was found in his mouth. When he was abused, he did not return abuse; when he suffered, he did not threaten; but he entrusted himself to the one who judges justly. He himself bore our sins in his body on the cross, so that, free from sins, we might live for righteousness; by his wounds you have been healed.'[99]

An eye for an eye

In his book *The Dignity of Difference: How to Avoid the Clash of Civilizations*, Jonathan Sacks engages with the thesis put forward by Samuel P. Huntington that future wars will be fought not between nation states but between cultures (see Chapter 1). Sacks observes how historic grievances are rarely forgotten and how retaliation is the instinctive response to perceived wrong. Families, communities and nations have long memories. We pass down to our children, and to our children's children, our unresolved agendas. Disaffection breeds bitterness and resentment and a desire for vengeance. In the short term, vindictive punishment may bring relief, but in the long term it generates a cycle of resentment and violence:

> The virus of hate can lie dormant for a while, but it rarely dies. Instead, it mutates ... Historic grievances are rarely forgotten. They become part of a people's collective memory, the narrative parents tell their children, the story from which a group draws its sense of identity. A note of injustice not yet avenged is written into the script which is then

re-enacted at moments of crisis. That is what makes conflict the default option between ancient antagonists, however many years of relative peace have intervened.[100]

Violence begets violence and part of Jonah's message may have been to denounce it in an attempt to break its destructive cycle. His story invites us to excavate our own violent desires and thoughts, and offer them to God in penitence. We do not know exactly what Jonah preached but we do know the *effect* of his preaching. His message is heard not only by the ordinary men and women in the street; it permeates the heart of the political establishment. 'And the people of Nineveh believed God; they proclaimed a fast, and everyone, great and small, put on sackcloth.'[101]

There is an interesting detail here that is only apparent in the original language. It relates to the use of the word 'God', *elohim*, rather than the Divine Name, Yahweh – the LORD. The people of Nineveh do not as yet know the God to whom they are responding. They cannot name him, but their ignorance does not invalidate their repentance. God still acknowledges their repentance and forgives them. The text is silent about whether their repentance turns into obedience to God's laws and whether in the long term they start to worship Yahweh. But something has clearly stirred in the hearts and minds of the Ninevites, even if it is only the first step in a longer process. For most people conversion is not a sudden, one-off event that comes out of the blue. Rather, it is a process of change and awakening. In the case of the Ninevites, it begins with an acknowledgement of their sin, recognizing that violence is destroying the fabric of their society. This realization leads to repentance, not merely in words, but with deeds – the violence stops. And this leads to some sort of acknowledgement of the sovereignty of God.

The sign of Jonah

'When God saw what [the Ninevites] did, how they turned from their evil ways, God changed his mind about the calamity that he had said he would bring upon them; and he did not do it.' In the canon of the Old Testament, the repentance of the Ninevites in response to the preaching of Jonah stands out in marked contrast to the indifference with which Israel habitually treated the pronouncements of its prophets. And this contrast would not have been wasted either on Jonah's contemporaries or on subsequent generations. It is why, of all the possible episodes in the Hebrew Scriptures, Jesus selects Jonah as the paramount 'sign' of his own ministry. He refers not only to Jonah in the belly of the fish, but also to the extraordinary repentance of the Ninevites. 'The people of Nineveh will rise up at the judgement with this generation and condemn it, because they repented at the proclamation of Jonah, and see something greater than Jonah is here.'[102] Jesus is highlighting the obstinacy of his own generation to respond to his teaching.

The story of Jonah rebukes anyone who presumes that God is on their side. The more one studies this book, the more one realizes that this is not a cosy fable about a man and a whale. It is a well-crafted, razor-sharp commentary on the failings of individuals and nations, undoubtedly written to rebuke complacency among the restored community of Jewish exiles and stimulate spiritual renewal. But it is also an affirmation of God's good purposes for humankind. From Jonah I learn that in the public square the call to repentance is best done by reflecting on 'the signs of our times', addressing social injustice and the things that fuel hatred and bitterness, which, if unaddressed, are likely to erupt into violence. We need the courage of Jonah to denounce what is wrong, but also the wisdom (in the words of St Paul) to identify and affirm all that is good, noble and true.[103] Otherwise, we are vulnerable to being ignored by our secular contemporaries or labelled as killjoys. Striking a balance between the call to repentance and the affirmation of goodness and achievement is an art form we should strive to acquire.

Here the teaching of another Hebrew prophet, Micah, may offer fertile ground. 'He has told you, O mortal, what is good; and what does the Lord require of you but to do justice, and to love kindness, and to walk humbly with your God?'[104] Justice, mercy and humility form a threefold path that many in our diverse and multicultural society may find their way to embracing. They designate a path wide and deep enough for Christian, Jew, Muslim, and those of no faith, to walk side by side and work for the common good.

Reflections

- Given 'the signs of our times', what are the things of which we should be repenting as a society? How might we frame God's call to repentance to our generation in which there will always be those 'who do not know their left hand from their right hand'? What are the achievements we should be affirming and celebrating?

- How do we break the cycles of violence and hatred, and the anger that foments just below the surface? What do we learn from Jesus's teaching and example?

- What are the things that have caused you to have violent thoughts or to be angry? How do you use them as the raw material for your prayer?

> Eternal Light, shine into our hearts.
> Eternal Goodness, deliver us from evil.
> Eternal Power, be our support.
> Eternal Wisdom, scatter the darkness of our ignorance.
> Eternal Pity, have mercy upon us;
> that with all our heart and mind and soul and strength
> we may seek your face and be brought by your
>   infinite mercy
> into your holy presence; through Jesus Christ our Lord.
>
> Alcuin of York (735–804)

Throughout your life, learn to trust in the providential care of God, through which alone comes contentment. Work hard, but always cooperate with God's good designs. Let me assure you, if you trust all to God, whatever happens will be the best for you, whether at the time it seems good or bad to your own judgement. God will work with you and in you and for you throughout your life. And at the last you will know that you have not laboured in vain and be filled with a profound contentment which only God can give.

Francis de Sales (1567–1622)
'Introduction to the Devout Life'

7
The God who provides

Undergirding the story of Jonah is a theology of providence. It describes a God who cares, who orders things and (most importantly) who provides. Even when Jonah messes up and is disobedient, God still provides for his needs. This is good news for we lesser mortals. It is not a 'get out of jail' card, as if Jonah can swan through life, immune from challenge and difficulty: God holds him responsible and persists in calling him. God is portrayed as One who does not give Jonah (or us) everything we want but does give us everything we need.

The language of this book is worthy of careful reflection. When Jonah is thrown overboard by the terrified crew, the reason he does not drown, or so we are told, is because God 'appoints' or 'provides' a gigantic fish to swallow him. Later, God will 'provide' a broom bush (or whatever it was) to grow up to shade him from the heat of the sun; and then 'provide' a worm to attack the bush so that it withers; and finally 'provide' a wind that will scorch the top of Jonah's exposed head and give him a thumping headache. Each time the same Hebrew verb 'to provide', *manah*, is used. It is the verb for arranging and governing, rather than for creating, and it presupposes that God is the sovereign disposer of all. But it does raise questions about how we understand God's action in the world. Do we believe God 'provides' things in life so that we are cared for in the way that Jonah was looked after or, to give another example from Scripture, the way angels sustained an exhausted Elijah with food and drink, 'otherwise the journey be too much for you'?[105]

At the end of the American Civil War, in the diary of an unknown Confederate soldier, this entry was discovered:

> I asked for strength that I might achieve;
> and I was made weak that I might learn humility.
> I asked for health that I might do great things;
> and I was given infirmity that I might do better things.
> I asked for riches that I might be happy;
> and I was given poverty that I might be wise.
> I asked for power that I might have the praise of men;
> and I was given weakness that I might feel my need
>   of God.
> I asked for all things that I might enjoy life,
> and I was given life that I might enjoy all things.
> I got nothing I had prayed for,
> but everything that I had hoped for.
> Almost despite myself,
> my unspoken prayers were answered;
> I am, among all men, most richly blessed.

Although God may not have given the soldier everything he had prayed for, he believed God had provided him with everything he genuinely needed, and as a result he felt blessed. The soldier had learned that prayer is not coercing God but being in communion with God. William Cowper's hymn 'God moves in a mysterious way', penned in the eighteenth century, reflects a similar understanding and contains these hallowed lines:

> Judge not the Lord by feeble sense,
> But trust him for his grace;
> Behind a frowning providence
> He hides a smiling face.

Cowper's words have brought solace to countless congregations, but is he expressing anything more than pious sentiment? Cynics say that the doctrine of providence provides preachers with a golden opportunity to indulge their favourite hobby: plugging the intellectual gaps in their sermons with devotional material. Admittedly, the doctrine is perched between two polarities: on the one hand, the need to vindicate the good purposes of God for his creation and, on the other hand, the need to secure the freedom and autonomy of humankind. But beneath its theological vaulting is a crevasse: the suspicion of divine incompetence. Is the doctrine of providence just 'wishful thinking'? There is ample material for both the philosopher of religion and the cynic to feast on and it may be that there is no satisfactory response to their criticisms; at least, not in this life. God's purposes, which Cowper doggedly declares to be 'unfolding every hour', may refuse to put in an appearance in the way we want. Worse, maybe there is no smiling face to perceive?

Providence

Providence derives from the Latin *providere*, meaning 'foresight'. In English we use the word to designate measures we put in place in the light of what we foresee. We 'provide' for a contingency or are 'provident' in the use of our money and resources. God's providence refers to what God foresees, and it applies both to his care for creation and to his provision for our needs and guidance. God acts towards his creation with the same purpose and in the same spirit in which he created it. This rebuts a view of God as remote, as an impassive bystander observing the plight of humankind; a benign but largely impotent God who has withdrawn to the touchlines of the universe from where he shouts words of encouragement to the exhausted players on the pitch. Augustine sets out his belief in God's good purposes powerfully and elegantly:

> God is the unchanging conductor as well as the unchanged creator of all things that change. When he adds, abolishes, curtails, increases or diminishes the rights of any age, he is ordering all events according to his providence until the beauty of the completed course of time, whose parts are the dispensations suitable to each different period, shall have played itself out like the great melody of some ineffable composer.[106]

Augustine pictures God as the source of stability, the still point in the turning world. God is both composer and conductor, creating music out of discordant voices. His thought chimes with the verse embroidered by my great-grandmother on her sampler, where God is pictured weaving not only the golden and silver threads of life into 'the pattern he has planned' but the dark threads too. The thought underlying both is essentially aesthetic, the creation of beauty and harmony. It is also reflected in the words of a fifth-century prayer ascribed to St Gelasius:

> O God of unchangeable power and eternal light,
> look favourably on your whole church,
> that wonderful and sacred mystery;
> and by the tranquil operation of your perpetual providence,
> carry out the work of our salvation;
> let the whole world feel and see
> that things which were cast down are being raised up,
> that those which had grown old are being made new,
> and that all things are returning to perfection;
> through him from whom they took their origin,
> even Jesus Christ our Lord. Amen.[107]

In all these examples, the doctrine of providence celebrates hope in the God who brings harmony, who is both the beginning and the end, the Alpha and Omega. Inevitably we find ourselves speaking and praying from a position somewhere in the middle of this cosmic alphabet and in a world that does not appear to be responding to the 'operation of God's perpetual providence'. 'Tranquil' may be St Gelasius's description for God's work, but it is not a word that readily comes to mind when discussing the 'signs of the times' and the turbulence of international affairs. Built into the fabric of our existence is a destructive randomness that seems to militate against the attainment of perfection. In the words of another ancient prayer, we are 'wearied by the changes and chances of this fleeting world' and long to 'repose upon God's eternal changelessness'. This is why the language of providence is best rooted in the realm of spirituality as we each search for meaning in our lives, 'seeking the poem in the pain', to borrow words of the Welsh poet R. S. Thomas.[108]

In that search we may decide to stick by William Cowper's words: 'God is his own interpreter / And he will make it plain.' No doubt God is, and no doubt he will. But the fact is *we* are in the business of interpretation too. In our bewilderment, when the 'right road is lost', we have no alternative but to try to interpret the opaqueness of our experience. We should resist carving up events into compartments labelled respectively 'divine' and 'human'. In this life we have only to deal with one kind of actions – human actions. This is not to deny the activity of God on earth or to question its potency, but it is to understand the agency of God behind and alongside human actions. Commenting on the providential care of God, the theologian T. H. L. Parker says:

> According to [God's] own eternal purpose he guides and makes his own use of human activity. This does not make human activity divine and therefore holy. It continues in all its humanity to be a source of pride or shame to the doer of it and it bears the praise or blame that human works deserve. Men act, and must act, in the human freedom that God has given them. It is in that freedom that God claims their obedience. Yet God does not fulfil his purpose only in men's obedient actions, but also in [their] careless and even downright rebellious deeds.[109]

In the struggle for interpretation, as we have noted, analogies and metaphors cluster round the notion of design: there is a pattern to be discerned, a poem to be discovered, a melody or harmony to be appreciated, a tapestry to be unfurled. This mesh of imagery is trying to make sense of the mixture of good and bad we experience. But is the alleged pattern 'there', awaiting our recognition, or is it something of our own making? Do we project a pattern on to the raw material of our experience because we are scared that there is no design to discover? To put it crudely: do we weave our own tapestry?

To that last question, I would answer yes. My 'yes' is not a negation of God, in whose hands lie all things, but an affirmation of the creativity that God shares with those made in his image. The Greek theologians of the early Christian centuries had a wonderful word for it: *synergia*, meaning joint energies. In their understanding, the doctrine of providence confronts not only a view of God as a passive spectator, but also the rival heresy of the impotence of humankind in the face of an omnipotent God. And this is where the image of tapestry comes alive, not as a means of resolving the ambivalence of our experience, but as an invitation to understand human and divine creativity. 'God will work with you and in you and for you throughout your life,' says St Francis de Sales. 'And at the last you will know that you have not laboured in vain and be filled with a profound contentment which only God can give.'[110]

Many years ago, when I was a university chaplain, I travelled with a group of undergraduates across Turkey into Armenia, and from there into Azerbaijan and Georgia. The north-east border between Turkey and Armenia has been disputed for centuries. That year, for the first time in decades, but sadly no longer, a train was permitted to cross the Turkish-Armenian border once a week. So it was, as we waited for the arrival of our train bound for Yerevan, the capital of Armenia, we found ourselves exploring Kars. The city was originally Armenian, but in imperial times it had become an outpost oscillating between the Russian tsars and the Ottoman Turks in their struggle to control the area. The city is home to a vast open-air market for carpets and rugs and, in spite of closed borders, nomadic families in the region manage to find their way to Kars to sell their wares.

The role of the women in these nomadic families is to collect the mosses and lichens which they boil up with root vegetables to create the distinctive red dyes used to colour the wool. The men weave the rugs on large portable looms. Successive generations of fathers teach their skills to their sons by giving them the freedom not only to observe, but to practise and learn. Periodically, the child makes a mistake: he fails to observe accurately the intricacies of the pattern his father is weaving. But the father, rather than unpick his son's work, incorporates the flaw into the design of the carpet, which, as a result, changes. The originality and beauty of each carpet is dependent not simply on the skill of the father, but on the mistakes of the son. It is another picture of the divine-human endeavour.

Søren Kierkegaard, the Danish philosopher, says: 'We live our lives forwards, but we understand them backwards.'[111] The doctrine of providence has meaning in retrospect, not prospect. It is only as we look back that we can see where we have travelled and (hopefully) discover meaning in our bewilderment and know that we have been blessed.

Reflections

- Do you believe God 'provides' things in life so that you are cared for in the way that Jonah was sustained throughout his life?

- Looking back on your life, can you think of an example where you see the 'operation of God's perpetual providence'?

- Compose a psalm or prayer of thanksgiving in celebration of your experience of the providence of God.

O God, you know us to be set
in the midst of so many and great dangers,
that by reason of the frailty of our nature
we cannot always stand upright:
grant to us such strength and protection
as may support us in all dangers
and carry us through all temptations;
through Jesus Christ our Lord.

Common Worship

One form of gentleness that we should all practise is towards ourselves. We should never get irritable with ourselves, fretting at our imperfections. It is entirely reasonable to be displeased and feel sorry when we have done something wrong, but we should refrain from being full of self-recrimination, fretful or spiteful to ourselves. Some people make the great mistake of being angry because they have been angry, hurt because they have allowed themselves to be hurt, vexed because they have allowed themselves to be vexed. They think that they are getting rid of their anger, that the second remedies the first; but they are trapped in a destructive cycle of emotion which will come to the surface in a fresh outburst of anger on a later occasion.

When your heart has fallen, raise it up softly, gently, humbling yourself before God, acknowledging your fault, but without being surprised at your fall. Human infirmity is infirmity; human weakness is weak; and human frailty is frail. Own your fault before God and return to the way of virtue which you had forsaken, with great courage and confidence in the mercy of God.

Francis de Sales
(1567–1622)
'Introduction to the
Devout Life'

8
The God of compassion and love

Our reluctant prophet has delivered his message to the people of Nineveh and it has been heard. You might think that Jonah would be delighted that the Ninevites had repented, and that God had shown clemency, but not at all. He has a terrible, petulant strop:

> When God saw what the [Ninevites] did, how they turned from their evil ways, God changed his mind about the calamity that he had said he would bring upon them; and he did not do it. But this was very displeasing to Jonah, and he became angry. He prayed to the LORD and said, 'O LORD! Is not this what I said while I was still in my own country? That is why I fled to Tarshish at the beginning; for I knew that you are a gracious God and merciful, slow to anger, and abounding in steadfast love, and ready to relent from punishing. And now, O LORD, please take my life from me, for it is better for me to die than to live.' And the LORD said, 'Is it right for you to be angry?' Then Jonah went out of the city and sat down east of the city, and made a booth for himself there. He sat under it in the shade, waiting to see what would become of the city.

The LORD God appointed a bush, and made it come up over Jonah, to give shade over his head, to save him from his discomfort; so Jonah was very happy about the bush. But when dawn came up the next day, God appointed a worm that attacked the bush, so that it withered. When the sun rose, God prepared a sultry east wind, and the sun beat down on the head of Jonah so that he was faint and asked that he might die. He said, 'It is better for me to die than to live.'

But God said to Jonah, 'Is it right for you to be angry about the bush?' And he said, 'Yes, angry enough to die.' Then the LORD said, 'You are concerned about the bush, for which you did not labour and which you did not grow; it came into being in a night and perished in a night. And should I not be concerned about Nineveh, that great city, in which there are more than a hundred and twenty thousand people who do not know their right hand from their left, and also many animals?'[112]

It is called sulking. We have all done it, particularly when we were young. We do it as adults too, except we are more subtle about it. Jonah has become obdurate. He is in a state of open rebellion against God. He is angry and embarrassed, perhaps concerned about his own reputation and whether he will be judged a false prophet because his words did not come true.[113] He recognizes that Yahweh has forgiven the Ninevites, and that God will not destroy their city as he had anticipated and hoped. He did not need a special revelation to grasp this because it is in accord with Yahweh's character and he vents his frustration: 'I knew that you are a God gracious and merciful, slow to anger, and abounding in steadfast love, and ready to relent from punishing.' Jonah resents God for being God, for being more merciful than he thinks the Ninevites deserve. Jonah wants a tribal god who is on his side and who will bash his enemies and rub their faces into the dirt.

Jonah's response is an instinctive universal human response to such events, but it is shot through with irony. Not long before, Jonah had suffered the trauma of being caught in a terrible storm, being thrown overboard and nearly drowning. He had been swallowed by a giant fish and, from its belly, complained bitterly about his predicament. Gradually his psalm of protest moved into the praise of God as it dawned on him that he was not going to die. Jonah knows God is merciful because he has experienced God's benevolence at first hand. What he cannot cope with is the thought that this same God might now act in an identical way to the Ninevites, these nasty, evil foreigners who delight in gratuitous violence. Instead of rejoicing in God's kindness and extravagant mercy, Jonah becomes angry; so angry, in fact, he says he wants to die.

I have to say that I am not unsympathetic to Jonah. I too find it difficult to get my mind round the fact that God loves other people as much as he loves me. How dare he? It's not fair. But grace isn't fair. This is why the Book of Jonah is so challenging. God is not limited by my perceptions and prejudices. Nor is God confined by national boundaries or religious tramlines. God has no favourites and, as Jesus will tell his disciples, 'makes his sun rise on the evil and on the good, and sends rain on the righteous and on the unrighteous'.[114] Preaching repentance and forgiveness involves the risk that God may not deal with others as we would wish. Forgiveness is unfair but it does free us from being trapped in an endless cycle of retribution.

The God of grace and mercy

'I knew you are a gracious God and merciful, slow to anger, and abounding in steadfast love, and ready to relent from punishing,' admits Jonah. The words have a formulaic ring to them. They are found eight times scattered through the Hebrew Scriptures and are echoed in at least seven other places, one of which is here in the Book of Jonah. Some scholars think that its formulaic style suggests that it originated in the liturgy of the Temple. The consensus among scholars is that the form of words in Exodus 34.6 is highly likely to be the original version from which other versions derive. It is a key text for Jew and Christian alike and is part of a longer passage in Exodus from which Jewish exegetes traditionally draw eleven attributes of God. In Jonah, four of these attributes are specifically mentioned: grace, mercy, long-suffering (or 'slow to anger' as it is translated here) and faithful love:

rachum, 'the merciful Being': God is tender and compassionate;
channun, 'the gracious One': the very nature of God is goodness and love;
'erech 'appayim, 'the One who is long-suffering and patient';
chesed, 'the One whose nature is steadfast love'.

To Jonah's frustration, the God of compassion and love has dealt kindly with the Ninevites. How does God respond to Jonah's petulance? Once again, God does not tell him off. Instead, God deals gently with him and asks: 'Are you right to be so angry?' The question invites self-reflection, and God addresses the same question to us. Anger is neutral. It is something we all experience from time to time. The question is: what do we do with it?

Managing our anger

I thought I was a nice person until I became a monk. It wasn't until I entered the monastery that I realized how much unresolved anger lodged inside me. In hindsight (and hindsight is a wonderful thing, as we all know) this should not have surprised me because monastic life is about the encounter of the self with God, and of necessity it includes facing oneself. But it was a shock all the same, and doubtless not a very pleasant experience for my brethren either. There is an old monastic joke that if ever there were to be a murder in a monastery the police would find it very difficult to identify the murderer because everyone in the community would have had a reason to bump off old Brother Sylvester. As a seasoned monk in a neighbouring monastery once said to me, 'It's not the vows that are the problem: it's the brethren.'

Dealing with anger is difficult for all of us, including monks. It is no coincidence that a lot of people's 'driven-ness' is fuelled by deeply buried anger. Anger and disappointment often go hand in hand and have a corrosive effect on our relationships. Things spoken in anger can't be un-said. Once you've said it, you've said it. What initially presents itself, however, may not be anger but jealousy of what others appear to have. If we deny our anger exists and bottle it up, it will eat away our insides and make us ill. When we repress anger, it sinks to the bottom of our consciousness and turns into depression.

It is worth remembering that the true opposite of love is not hatred but indifference, which is why anger can be an expression of love and a sign of psychological health. This is not the same thing as saying we have a divine dispensation to go round punching people on the nose, claiming – as we do – that our anger is justified and in some spurious way 'righteous'. 'Be angry, but do not sin,' insists Paul when writing to the Ephesians. 'Do not let the sun go down on your anger, and do not make room for the devil.'[115] Or to return to the psalms: 'Let go of anger and abandon wrath. Do not fret. It will only lead you to do evil.'[116] First, we need to give ourselves permission to feel our anger; then we need to decide how best to manage it. If we don't manage our anger appropriately, we will end up either ill or in court or both.

For religious people, the management of anger will include turning it into prayer. St Francis de Sales, writing at the beginning of the seventeenth century, is wise when he says:

> Some people make the great mistake of being angry because they have been angry, hurt because they have allowed themselves to be hurt, vexed because they have allowed themselves to be vexed. They think that they are getting rid of their anger, that the second remedies the first; but they are trapped in a destructive cycle of emotion which will come to the surface in a fresh outburst of anger on a later occasion.[117]

With God's help, we need to develop the capacity to hold more than one emotion at any given time: anger *and* love. There is no easy route to emotional maturity, and it may be that, in a culture where we are expected to be happy all the time, allowing ourselves to feel sadness or to be angry is a step on the road to sanity. If we are not prepared to own our aggression, then this element of our humanity will be left unredeemed and poison our lives. We need to embrace our aggression and our capacity to be forceful and bring it into our prayer so that God can recruit our passion in creative ways, not least in the service of justice.

Jonah wants a God who is an extension of himself. Instead, Yahweh reveals himself as a God of immense and generous compassion. In theory, the focus of the book is the unexpected repentance of the Ninevites but, when we think about it, the person who is actually converted is Jonah, as the close of the book implies. We are treated to another miraculous story, this time about a bush – no one is certain of the identity of the plant the Hebrew refers to. The story has strong similarities with that recorded about the prophet Elijah, who also fled from God, sat down under a broom tree and wished for death.[118]

At the command of God, a bush grows up to provide Jonah with shade from the burning heat of the sun. Jonah is grateful for its protection, but then a worm attacks the roots of the bush, and it shrivels and dies. A sultry wind blows on Jonah, giving him a terrible headache. Exposed to the midday sun and exhausted by the heat, he becomes fretful and goes into an even deeper sulk. Once again, he says he wants to die. And once again God asks him: 'Are you right to be so angry?' 'Yes,' he says defiantly, and we see how ludicrous his response is and (with luck) we laugh, recognizing our own foibles. It is a lovely comic episode with which to conclude the book, but there is wisdom in this exchange, not just humour.

Compunction of heart

Like most churches, synagogues operate a lectionary: a systematic way of reading the Scriptures in their worship. Repentance and deliverance are the dominant themes in Jonah, which is why Jews read the book in its entirety during the afternoon service on the holy day of Yom Kippur, the Day of Atonement. The Christian tradition similarly sees the Book of Jonah as a story of repentance and compunction. Compunction is not a word we hear much today, but it makes regular appearances in early monastic literature.

Compunction was a medical term used by the Roman doctors to describe episodes of acute pain. The Latin word *punctio*, from which it derives and from which we get our words 'puncture' and 'punctuate', designated a sharp pricking or stabbing pain. The early Christian monastics adopted this medical term and applied it to pain of the spirit, a pricking of the conscience, a remorse born of penitence. The term tallies with the advice of Cardinal Newman: 'It is often said that second thoughts are best; so they are in matters of judgment, but not in matters of conscience.'[119]

Feelings of regret, remorse and self-contempt are evidence of an active conscience. They are emotions we all experience from time to time. Compunction of heart – *compunctio cordis* – is different. It describes a radical openness to God which makes possible a moment of profound disclosure. Falsity and illusion are stripped away, and the human heart is pierced by a perception of the truth that leads to liberation. The Desert Fathers and Mothers said that the first sign of this happening in someone's life is the presence of tears. God's love punctures our self-conceit as if it were a spiritual cyst and we weep. In our culture, tears are invariably seen as an embarrassment, a sign of weakness, certainly for men. Big men don't cry. Our forebears viewed tears differently. They saw tears as a gift from God. Far from being a sign that something is wrong, tears are evidence of the work of the Holy Spirit in a person's life. Something is going right: healing is taking place. An inner abscess has been lanced. Carol Ann Duffy alludes to this experience in her poem 'Prayer':

> Some nights, although we are faithless, the truth
> enters our hearts, that small familiar pain;
> then a man will stand stock-still, hearing his youth
> in the distant Latin chanting of a train.[120]

'The truth enters our hearts'. Compunction of heart. In Carol Ann Duffy's poem, the experience is not at all churchy or religious but is triggered unexpectedly by the sound of a train in the distance, perhaps eliciting a forgotten conversation or the memory of a painful betrayal. For Jonah, the experience was triggered by the death of a bush and his exposure to the heat of the sun.

Praying with creation

The Book of Jonah ends with the humbling of Jonah and a powerful but unexpected speech from God:

'You are concerned about the bush, for which you did not labour and which you did not grow; it came into being in a night and perished in a night. And should I not be concerned about Nineveh, that great city, in which there are more than a hundred and twenty thousand people who do not know their right hand from their left, and also many animals?'[121]

Or, as the King James Bible puts it so beautifully, 'and much cattle'.

In theory God's question is addressed to Jonah but in reality it is addressed to the reader – to us. We find ourselves no longer readers of a fable: we are participants in a drama. We are challenged to respond. We learn not only that God's love is not confined to the Jews; it is not even confined to human beings. In our arrogance, we think we are the only important creatures on the planet. We are not. God's love embraces plants and animals and the entire created order.

The sense of humankind being part of creation, and not apart from it, finds expression in the spirituality of many early Christian teachers. Tertullian, for example, in his treatise *On Prayer*, says:

> All creation prays. Cattle and wild beasts pray and bend their knees. As they come from their barns and caves they invariably look up to heaven and call out, lifting up their spirit in their own fashion. The birds too rise and lift themselves up to heaven: instead of hands, they open out their wings in the form of a cross and give voice to what seems to be a prayer.[122]

Writing in the fourth century, Gregory of Nazianzus says:

> All creatures praise you,
> both those who speak and those that are dumb.
> All creatures bow down before you,
> both those that can think and those that cannot.
> The longing of the universe,
> the groaning of creation reaches out to you.
> Everything that exists prays to you,
> and every creature that can read your universe
> directs to you a hymn of silence.[123]

An unexpected side-effect of the current ecological crisis has been the recovery of this ancient perspective. I see it reflected in the paintings of the crucifixion by Craigie Aitchison (1926–2009). His paintings have a childlike quality that I think is profound. The background of his paintings tends to be a dark palette of sombre purple hills, drab olive-green foregrounds with a menacing dark-blue sky overhead, and soil that is brown verging on black. The landscape he paints is invariably empty and stylized, but it gives a powerful focus to the cross and to the figure of Jesus draped over it. In all his paintings the figure of Christ has a translucent quality about it as if the light emanates from the Crucified One. The light of the world is dying, and the earth itself is going into mourning. One feature that recurs in his paintings of the crucifixion is the presence of animals. Mary the mother of Jesus and John the beloved disciple, who by tradition are usually represented standing at the foot of the cross, have disappeared. In Craigie's painting of the crucifixion in Tate Britain, it is not the centurion or a group of women that gaze up at the face of Christ, but a little dog, his own Bedlington terrier. It leans forward, puzzled, almost in conversation with the dying Jesus. Two little birds perch on the arm of the cross, watching. When asked about this, Craigie said that the creation alone had the innocence and the perception to bear witness to the magnitude of Christ's death. The cross represents humankind's extraordinary capacity for destructive selfishness, which is happy to destroy truth, beauty and, ultimately, life itself.

The prophet Jeremiah similarly talks about the earth going into mourning for the sins of the people, and of creation weeping the tears that humanity refuses to shed.[124] Here in the story of Jonah, God is revealed as intimately involved with all of creation, from the seas, the great sea monsters and all that swim in the deep, to the plants, trees and animals. Delighting in God and delighting in God's creation brings us fully alive as women and men, as the seventeenth-century Anglican divine Thomas Traherne writes:

> You never enjoy the world aright till the sea itself floweth in your veins, till you are clothed with the heavens, and crowned with the stars, and perceive yourself to be the sole heir of the whole world, and more than so, because men are in it who are every one sole heirs as well as you. Till you can sing and rejoice and delight in God, as misers do in gold, and kings in sceptres, you never enjoy the world. Till your spirit filleth the whole world, and the stars are your jewels; till you are as familiar with the ways of God in all ages as with your walk and table; till you are intimately acquainted with that shady nothing out of which the world was made; till you love men so as to desire their happiness with a thirst equal to the zeal of your own; till you delight in God for being good to all: you never enjoy the world.[125]

Reflections

- 'I knew you are a gracious God and merciful, slow to anger, and abounding in steadfast love, and ready to relent from punishing.' In what ways have you experienced this in your own life?

- How do you manage anger in your life? What are the triggers that you need to watch out for?

- Have you had an experience of compunction and unexpectedly found the truth entering your heart? What did you learn from it? How did the experience change you?

- What has the prophet Jonah taught you?

O Holy Spirit,
whose presence is liberty,
grant us that freedom of the spirit
which will not fear to travel your unknown ways,
nor be held back by misgivings of ourselves or fear
  of others.
Ever beckon us forward to the place of your will
which is also the place of your power,
O ever-leading, ever-loving Lord.

Source unknown

Let us sing 'Alleluia' here and now in this life, even though we are oppressed by various worries, so that we may sing it one day in the world to come when we are set free from all anxiety. Let us sing as travellers sing on a journey to help them keep on walking. Lighten your toil by singing and never be idle. Sing, my friends, and above all keep on walking.

Augustine (354–430)
Sermon 256

Epilogue

If Christianity is merely a human enterprise, then the darkness and sadness we each encounter on our journey through life will be just that – darkness. But the Book of Jonah encourages us to re-label these bewildering episodes as places of transformation. When a caterpillar pupates, nothing seems to be happening, but inside a butterfly is being formed. Spiritual metamorphosis may be too strong an image to describe what can be a succession of profoundly disorienting and painful experiences, but it has the merit of reminding us that discipleship is a process of growth, and growth necessarily involves change. As Dante says, there are good things to be discovered when we are lost in 'dark woods'.

Jonah is an open-ended book. Unusually, it concludes not with a statement but a question – in fact the last in a series of questions. Some of its questions are spoken, others are implied, and they punctuate the story of this reluctant prophet. They will have challenged the author's contemporaries, and they challenge us too. They bid us be alert and not complacent. They witness to an understanding of God as the God of all people and nations, a gracious God who cares for all creation, a God who calls us and our society to account. Which is why, in the words of Jesus, we need to read 'the signs of our times'. At times the task is daunting, but in all our struggles we have cause for joy because Jonah's story also witnesses to a God who is actively seeking our friendship, a God who is forbearing, merciful, gentle and unfailingly generous.

O that today we would hear his voice.

Acknowledgement of Copyright Sources

The Author and Publisher are grateful for permission to reproduce material under copyright and in particular to:

Faber & Faber, for two quotations of T. S. Eliot, one from 'Choruses from "The Rock"' in *The Waste Land and Other Poems*, and the other from 'Little Gidding' in *Four Quartets*; and for Stevie Smith's poem 'Not Waving but Drowning' in *The Collected Poems and Drawings of Stevie Smith*, 2015.

New Directions Publishing Corp., for permission to reproduce Stevie Smith's poem 'Not Waving but Drowning', *All the Poems*, copyright ©1937, 1938, 1942, 1950, 1957, 1962, 1966, 1971, 1972 by Stevie Smith; copyright © 2016 by the Estate of James MacGibbon; copyright © 2015 by Will May.

Pan Macmillan, for lines from 'Prayer' by Carol Ann Duffy, in *Meantime*, subsequently reprinted in *New Selected Poems 1984–2004*.

The Author and Publisher would be grateful if any omissions or inaccuracies in these acknowledgements could be brought to their attention for correction.

List of Illustrations

Page x   Medieval Bible, c. 13th–14th century, https://commons.wikimedia.org.
Page xiii   Frescos, 14th century, catacombs of the Church of Marcellinus and Peter, Rome, https://commons.wikimedia.org.
Page xvi   Altar, 12th century, Klosterneuburg Abbey, Austria, https://commons.wikimedia.org.
Page 20   Wall mosaic, 12th century, St Mark's Basilica, Venice, https://commons.wikimedia.org.
Page 40   Forest paths, https://www.istockphoto.com.
Page 56   Mosaic floor, c. 5th century, synagogue overlooking the Sea of Galilee, https://commons.wikimedia.org.
Page 70   Ceramic tile, https://www.esotericmeanings.com.
Page 82   Relief of Assyrian soldiers holding spears, 7th century BCE, https://www.istockphoto.com.
Page 83   Artist's impression of Assyrian palaces, Sir Austen Henry Layard, 1849, *The Monuments of Nineveh*, London: John Murray, https://en.wikipedia.org.
Page 94   Medieval Bible, 13th–14th century, https://commons.wikimedia.org.
Page 104   Gothic stained glass, 13th century, detail of the Redemption Window in Canterbury Cathedral, https://commons.wikimedia.org.
Page 118   Fresco, 15th century, Härkeberga Church, Sweden, https://commons.wikimedia.org.

Notes

1 Murray, Paul, 2002, *A Journey with Jonah: The Spirituality of Bewilderment*, Dublin: The Columba Press.
2 Bolt, Robert, 1969, *A Man for All Seasons*, London: Heinemann, Act 2.
3 2 Corinthians 12.12.
4 John 6.30.
5 Matthew 16.3.
6 Dodds, E. R., 1965, *Pagan and Christian in an Age of Anxiety*, Cambridge, New York and London: Cambridge University Press, p. 3. See also Brown, Peter, 1971, *The World in Late Antiquity*, New York: Harcourt Brace Jovanovich.
7 For discussion of social capital and what generates it, see Putnam, R. D., 2001, *Bowling Alone*, New York and London: Simon & Schuster.
8 Huntington, Samuel, P., 1992, *The Clash of Civilizations and the Remaking of World Order*, New York and London: Simon & Schuster.
9 Naisbitt, John, and Aburdene, Patricia, 1990, *Megatrends 2000*, London: Sidgwick & Jackson.
10 Eliot, T. S., 'Choruses from "The Rock"', *The Waste Land and Other Poems*, London: Faber & Faber, 1940.
11 The phrase coined by Sir Robert Armstrong, the British Cabinet Secretary, when giving evidence in the 'Spycatcher trial' in 1986.
12 These are the findings of the Public Inquiry into the Hillsborough football crowd control disaster in the UK in 1989, published in 2024, which was subtitled 'the patronising disposition of unaccountable power'.
13 https://blogs.lse.ac.uk/medialse/2018/11/22/truth-trust-and-technology-so-whats-the-problem/ (accessed 15.1.2025).
14 Ephesians 6.10–20.
15 1 Corinthians 13.12.
16 1 John 3.2.

17 *The Declaration of Independence*, in Congress, 4 July 1776, https://history.state.gov/milestones/1776-1783/declaration (accessed 15.1.2025).
18 Locke's works on *Toleration* (1689), *Human Understanding* (1690), *Civil Government* (1690) and *Education* (1693) have become foundation documents of the English liberal tradition.
19 According to the NSPCC and the Children's Society, the number of children in England needing treatment for serious mental health problems rose by 39% in a year. Referrals for specialist treatment rose from 839,570 in 2020–21 to 1.1 million in 2021–22. Dr Elaine Lockhart, chair of the Child and Adolescent Psychiatry Faculty at the Royal College of Psychiatrists, says that these statistics cover the whole range of mental health problems in children, ranging from those who are suicidal, self-harming and have eating disorders to those who experience serious depression, anxiety or addiction.
20 Haidt, Jonathan, 2024, *The Anxious Generation: How the Great Rewiring of Childhood is Causing an Epidemic of Mental Illness*, New York and London: Allen Lane, p. 27.
21 Haidt, *The Anxious Generation*, p. 14.
22 de Botton, Alain, 2004, *Status Anxiety*, New York and London: Penguin, pp. 3–4.
23 See Schwartz, B., 2004, *The Paradox of Choice: Why More is Less*, London and New York: HarperCollins.
24 See Newell, Benjamin, Lagnado, David, and Shanks, David, 2007, *Straight Choices: The Psychology of Decision Making*, London: Psychology Press.
25 Isaiah 55.2.
26 1 Timothy 6.19–20.
27 John 10.10.
28 Psalm 23.6.
29 Merton, Thomas, 1958, *Thoughts in Solitude*, Tunbridge Wells: Burns & Oates, p. 82.
30 Jeremiah 6.16.
31 Wills, Lawrence M., 1995, *The Jewish Novel in the Ancient World*, Ithaca, New York and London: Cornell University Press.
32 Luther, Martin, 1525, 'Lectures on Jonah: The German Text, 1525', in Luther, Martin, 1883–2009, *D. Martin Luthers Werke: Kritische Gesammtausgabe*, Weimar: Herman Böhlau, vol. 19, pp. 185–251.
33 See Exodus 3.15 and Isaiah 42.8.
34 Exact numbers of deportees are impossible to know. Different figures are quoted in 2 Kings 24–25 and Jeremiah 52.28–30.

35 An Aramaism is an idiom of the Aramaic language, the presence of which in the biblical Hebrew text may indicate the date of a book. See Eames, Christopher, 2022, 'Aramaic in the Book of Jonah: Evidence of Late Authorship? Or Something Else Entirely?', 12 November, Armstrong Institute of Biblical Archaeology, https://armstronginstitute.org/789-aramaic-in-the-book-of-jonah-evidence-of-late-authorship-or-something-else-entirely (accessed 15.1.2025).
36 See Psalms 89.38–51.
37 Jonah 1.1–3.
38 Nahum 3.1, 19.
39 Nahum 1.15.
40 Halton, Charles, 2008, 'How Big Was Nineveh? Literal Versus Figurative Interpretation of City Size', *Bulletin for Biblical Research*, 18(2), pp. 193–207.
41 Francis Thompson's 'The Hound of Heaven' was first printed in 1890 in the periodical *Merry England*, later to appear in Thompson's first collection of poetry, *Poems*, in 1893, London: Elkin Mathews & John Lane.
42 Psalm 139.1–10.
43 Jeremiah 23.24.
44 1 Corinthians 13.12.
45 Jonah 1.4–17.
46 Matthew 8.23–27.
47 Cited from Igumen Chariton of Valamo, 1966, *The Art of Prayer: An Orthodox Anthology*, trans. Kadloubovsky, E., and Palmer, E. M., ed. Ware, Timothy, London: Faber & Faber, p. 143.
48 Hopkins, Gerard Manley, 'No Worst, There Is None', in Hardner, W. H., and MacKenzie, N. II., eds., 1970, *The Poems of Gerard Manley Hopkins*, 4th edition, London: Oxford University Press, p. 100.
49 *King Lear*, III. 4.
50 *Carmen de Jona et Ninive*, 1112, *Tertulliani Opera Omnia, Tomus Posterior*, ed., 1866, Paris: PL 2, col. 1170.
51 Robinson, Marilynne, 2024, *Reading Genesis*, New York & London: Virago, p. 19.
52 Isaiah 43.1–3a.
53 Bonhoeffer, Dietrich, 1937, *The Cost of Discipleship*, Munich; English translation, 1959, London: SCM Press, p. 79.
54 Matthew 7.7.
55 Eliot, T. S., 1942, 'Little Gidding', *Four Quartets*, London: Faber & Faber.
56 Maitland, David, 1985, *Looking Both Ways: A Theology for Mid-life*, Louisville: Westminster John Knox Press, p. 1.

57 Jung, C. G., 1971, in Jacobi, J., ed., *Psychological Reflections: A New Anthology of His Writings*, London: Routledge, pp. 137f.
58 Merton, *Thoughts in Solitude*, p. 81.
59 Frost, Robert, 'The Road Not Taken', first published in the August 1915 issue of the *Atlantic Monthly*; later published as first poem in 1916 poetry collection *Mountain Interval*, New York: Henry Holt.
60 As quoted in Plato, *Cratylus*, 402a.
61 Hilary of Poitiers, *On the Trinity*, 1, 1-7.
62 1 Timothy 6.18-19.
63 Cicero, *Laelius: On Friendship*, 6.
64 Deuteronomy 30.15, 19-20.
65 Augustine, *The City of God*, 14.
66 Psalm 38.9.
67 Isaiah 30.20-21.
68 Dante Alighieri, *Inferno*, Canto 1.
69 Jonah 1.17-2.10.
70 Cassian, John, *Conferences*, 10, 11.
71 *King Lear*, V. 3.
72 Bennett, Alan, 2004, *The History Boys*, London: Faber & Faber.
73 Psalm 3.8.
74 de Caussade, Jean-Pierre, *Abandonment to Divine Providence*, 6, 5.
75 Smith, Martin, 1991, *A Season for the Spirit*, London: HarperCollins, pp. 16f.
76 John 4.14.
77 John 7.37-39.
78 Smith, Stevie, 1983, 'Not Waving but Drowning', in *The Collected Poems and Drawings of Stevie Smith*, London: Faber & Faber; and also 1983, *Collected Poems of Stevie Smith*, New York: New Directions Publishing Corporation, pp. 393-6.
79 Cunningham, Michael, 1998, *The Hours*, London and New York: HarperCollins, p. 98.
80 Blake, William, 'Auguries of Innocence', trans. Dante, Gabriel Rossetti, 1863.
81 Isaiah 50.10 (author's own translation).
82 Genesis 32.22.
83 Jonah 3.1-10.
84 Julian of Norwich, *Revelations of Divine Love*, 1966, trans. Wolters, Clifton, London: Penguin Books.
85 Jonah 3.2.

86 Halton, 'How Big Was Nineveh?' See also Eames, Christopher, February 2021, 'Jonah's Remarkably Accurate Account of Assyria', Armstrong Institute of Biblical Archaeology, https://armstronginstitute.org/312-jonahs-remarkably-accurate-account-of-assyria (accessed 3.3.2025).
87 Jonah 3.4.
88 Balawat was a city near Nineveh.
89 See Halton, 'How Big Was Nineveh?'
90 Jonah 3.8.
91 Genesis 4.
92 Genesis 6.13.
93 Psalms 11.5; 55; 58.2; 72.14; 73.6; 74.20; Proverbs 4.17; 10.6, 11; 13.2; 21.7; 24.2.
94 Psalm 137.9.
95 Isaiah 60.18.
96 Luke 9.54.
97 Matthew 26.51; Mark 14.47; Luke 18.10; John 18.10.
98 Matthew 26.52.
99 1 Peter 2.21-24.
100 Sacks, Jonathan, 2002, *The Dignity of Difference: How to Avoid the Clash of Civilizations*, London, New York and Sydney: Continuum, p. 178.
101 Jonah 3.5.
102 Matthew 12.41.
103 Philippians 4.8.
104 Micah 6.8.
105 1 Kings 19.4-8.
106 Augustine, *Letter* 138, 1, 5.
107 *Gelasian Sacramentary*, trans. Bright, William, 1861.
108 Thomas, R. S., 1972, 'Petition', *H'm*, London: Macmillan.
109 Parker, T. H. L., 1969, 'Providence', in Richardson, A., *Dictionary of Christian Theology*, London: SCM Press, p. 281.
110 Sales, Francis de, 1988, 'Introduction to the Devout Life', trans. Péronne, Marie Thibert, in Wright, Wendy M., ed., *Francis de Sales, Jane de Chantal: Letters of Spiritual Direction*, Classics of Western Spirituality, New York: Paulist Press, pp. 3, 9.
111 Kierkegaard, Søren, 1843, *Journals*, IV, A, 164.
112 Jonah 3.10-4.11.
113 Deuteronomy 18.21-22.
114 Matthew 5.45.
115 Ephesians 4.26.

116 Psalm 37.8.
117 Sales, 'Introduction to the Devout Life', pp. 3, 9.
118 1 Kings 19.4.
119 Newman, John Henry, 1909, *Parochial and Plain Sermons*, vol. 4, London: Longmans, Green, & Co., p. 36.
120 Duffy, Carol Ann, 2004, 'Prayer', first published in *Meantime*, subsequently in *New Selected Poems 1984–2004*, London: Picador/Macmillan, p. 129.
121 Jonah 4.10–11.
122 Tertullian, *On Prayer*, 29.
123 Gregory of Nazianzus, *Dogmatic Poems*, 29.
124 Jeremiah 12.11; 14.2.
125 Traherne, Thomas, *Centuries of Meditations*, I, paras 28–30, from Inge, Denise, ed., 2002, *Thomas Traherne: Poetry and Prose*, London: SPCK, p. 4.